D0810738

# The Theatre of E. E. Cummings

# The Theatre
## of
# E. E. Cummings

Edited and with an introduction by

George Firmage

*With an afterword by Norman Friedman*

LIVERIGHT PUBLISHING CORPORATION

A Division of W. W. Norton & Company

New York · London

For information about permission to reproduce selections from this book,
write to Permissions, Liveright Publishing Corporation,
a division of W. W. Norton & Company, Inc.,
500 Fifth Avenue, New York, NY 10110

For information about special discounts for bulk purchases, please contact
W. W. Norton Special Sales at specialsales@wwnorton.com or 800-233-4830

Manufacturing by RR Donnelley Harrisonburg
Book design by Dana Sloan
Production manager: Julia Druskin

ISBN 978-0-87140-654-5

Liveright Publishing Corporation
500 Fifth Avenue, New York, N.Y. 10110
www.wwnorton.com

W. W. Norton & Company Ltd.
Castle House, 75/76 Wells Street, London W1T 3QT

1 2 3 4 5 6 7 8 9 0

# Contents

# Introduction

Edmund Wilson, in his review of the Provincetown Playhouse production of *Him* for the *New Republic,* called it "the outpouring of an intelligence, a sensibility, and an imagination of the very first dimension. Cummings' characters speak with the true lifelike relief of comic genius." When the published version of the play first appeared in November 1927, the literary critics were, almost to a man, in agreement with Mr. Wilson's sentiments. However, when the theatre in Greenwich Village opened its doors on the evening of April 18, 1928, for the first performance of Cummings' work, the New York drama critics, with two notable exceptions (Mr. Wilson and John Anderson of the New York *Journal*), panned the play unmercifully. *Him* might be considered one of the first successful attempts at what is now called "the theatre of the absurd."

It might be helpful for the reader encountering *Him* for the very first time to have before him two items that appeared on the jacket of the first edition. The first, on the inside front flap of the jacket, was an "Imaginary Dialogue Between the Author and a Public as Imagined by E. E. Cummings":

AUTHOR: Well?

PUBLIC: What is *Him* about?

AUTHOR: Why ask me? Did I or didn't I make the play?

PUBLIC: But you surely know what you're making—

AUTHOR: Beg pardon, Mr. Public; I surely make what I'm knowing.

PUBLIC: So far as I'm concerned, my very dear sir, nonsense isn't everything in life.

AUTHOR: And so far as you're concerned "life" is a verb of two voices—active, to do, and passive, to dream. Others believe doing to be only a kind of dreaming. Still others have discovered (in a mirror surrounded by mirrors), something harder than silence but softer than falling; the third voice of "life," which believes itself and which cannot mean because it is.

PUBLIC: Bravo, but are such persons good for anything in particular?

AUTHOR: They are good for nothing except walking upright in the cordial revelation of the fatal reflexive.

PUBLIC: And your play is all about one of these persons, Mr. Author?

AUTHOR: Perhaps. But (let me tell you a secret) I rather hope my play is one of these persons.

The second item, a "thumbnail-analysis" that Cummings considered "an A1 job," appeared on the inside back flap of the jacket. Written by Isidor Schneider, a "poet in the advertising department" of the book's publisher, it offered "A Statement to a Certain Public by a Certain Publisher":

*There is good reason for Mr. Cummings' crypticism in his description of* Him. *We do not remember any book that more baffles an attempt to describe it.*

*You may think you know what to expect in a play by Cummings—and you will find out that you don't know the half of it. Such lucid madness, such adventurous gayety, such graceful irrever-*

*ence, such abounding novelties—squads of characters firing broad-sides of wit—interpolations of American folklore, extravagances that astound the imagination. It is a play that satisfies the five senses, and every corner of the intelligence—a play full of revels for the grown-up mind.*

Schneider's "Statement" might also serve to introduce the other works collected for the first time in this book. *Anthropos: or the Future of Art* first appeared in 1930 as a contribution to *Whither, Whither, or After Sex What? A Symposium to End Symposiums,* edited by Walter S. Hankel. In 1944 it was issued in a handsome limited edition of 222 copies by the Golden Eagle Press. To my knowledge it has never been performed on the professional stage.

*Santa Claus, A Morality* was first published in the Spring 1946 issue of *The Harvard Wake,* the "Cummings Number" of this short-lived periodical. In December 1946 the play appeared in a limited signed edition of 250 copies and an unlimited trade edition. It received its first professional "reading" on the stage of the Theatre de Lys, New York City, in the early 1960's.

*Tom,* the most wrongfully neglected work by E. E. Cummings, was published in October 1935 in a first and only edition of 1500 copies. George Freedley, Curator of the Theatre Collection, New York Public Library, wrote in *Stage Magazine*:

*The knowledgeable quality of his directions for movement will give the proper* régisseur *the keynote of the production. It presents the dancers and actors with a demand that they must strive to meet, for certainly* Tom *is meant to be staged. Marry the American ballet to the inspired group of negroes who made* Four Saints in Three Acts *a minor masterpiece. Then add a full symphony orchestra, a group of understanding actors, a designer as imaginative as Donald Oenslager or Stewart Chaney. To all these must be brought a direc-*

*tor who acknowledges the varied and sunning arts of the modern theatre, and can master them. Then it would make a performance that would thrill not only a New York but an American audience from the first tiara to the last standee. Mr. Cummings has made a working script which challenges the theatre to produce its best.*

"The challenge," writes Cummings' biographer Charles Norman, "so far as *Tom* is concerned, has not been taken up; it will be recalled, however, that a ballet about Uncle Tom was one of the most enchanting episodes in the Broadway success, *The King and I*, some fifteen years later. A complete score for *Tom* exists, the work of the composer David Diamond."

It is to be hoped that *The Theatre of E. E. Cummings* will reach a wide audience of performers as well as readers. For while the perceptive reader can stage a play or a ballet in his mind's eye, a performance will add that major dimension that is so much a part of all that E. E. Cummings created: LIFE!

*George J. Firmage*
*London, April 1967*

# HIM

looking forward into the past or looking
backward into the future I
walk on the highest
hills and
I laugh
about
it
all
the way

**ANNE BARTON**

# ACT ONE

## Scene I

SCENE: *A flat surface on which is painted a* DOCTOR *anaesthetizing a* WOMAN. *In this picture there are two holes corresponding to the heads of the physician and of the patient, and through these holes protrude the living heads of a man and of a woman.*

*Facing this picture, with their backs to the audience, three withered female* FIGURES *are rocking in rocking chairs and knitting.*

FIRST OR MIDDLE FIGURE: We called our hippopotamus It's Toasted.

SECOND OR FIGURE TO THE AUDIENCE'S RIGHT: I wish my husband didn't object to them.

THIRD: Of course it's a bother to clean the cage every day.

SECOND: O I wouldn't mind doing that.

FIRST: Be sure to get one that can sing.

THIRD: Don't they all sing?

FIRST: O dear no. Some of them just whistle.

SECOND: I've heard they're very affectionate.

FIRST: I find them so.

THIRD: Did it take long to tame yours?

FIRST: Only a few days. Now he sits on my hand and doesn't bite me.

SECOND: How charming.

THIRD: Is it true they imitate policemen?

FIRST: My dear they imitate everybody.

SECOND: I'm afraid my husband wouldn't like that.

FIRST: What do you mean, my dear?

SECOND: If ours imitated a policeman.

3

THIRD: Really? Why should he object?

SECOND: It would make him nervous I'm afraid—the idea of the thing.

FIRST: Your husband is a vegetarian?

SECOND: On the contrary, my husband is a burglar.

FIRST: Oh, I see. *(The* WOMAN'S *eyes close and her head remains in the picture; the* DOCTOR'S *head disappears from the picture leaving a hole. The three* FIGURES *continue to rock and knit. Presently the* DOCTOR *himself enters with* HIM.*)*

DOCTOR *(To* HIM*)*: Have a cigar. *(Produces two, one of which* HIM *takes. Both men bite off and spit out the tips of their cigars.* HIM, *producing matches, lights the* DOCTOR'S *and his own cigar.)* And how are the three Miss Weirds today?

FIRST FIGURE *(Without looking up or turning, continues knitting and rocking)*: Very well indeed, thank you doctor.

SECOND *(Ditto)*: Fine weather, isn't it?

THIRD *(Ditto)*: One really is glad to be alive.

DOCTOR: Speaking of dust, let me introduce a distinguished foreigner. Mr. Anybody, press flesh with the three Weird sisters; get used to Miss Stop, Miss Look and Miss Listen. (HIM *doubtfully extends his hand in the general direction of the unnoticing rocking and knitting* FIGURES*)*

FIRST FIGURE *(Snobbishly, to* SECOND*)*: I don't think I ever heard the name. *(To* THIRD*)*: Did you? *(All three* FIGURES *shake their heads)*

HIM: Madam, I am very noble.

DOCTOR: "Anybody" is just his nomb D.ploom you know. My friend is strictly incog.

FIRST FIGURE *(Stops knitting and rocking)*: How romantic!

SECOND *(Ditto)*: How thrilling!

THIRD *(Ditto)*: Do tell us his real name!

HIM: My real name, ladies, is Everyman, Marquis de la Poussière.

FIRST FIGURE *(Rising, turns; revealing a mask face)*: Delighted, Marquis.

SECOND *(Rising, turns; revealing a mask face identical with the* FIRST'S*)*: Enchanted.

THIRD *(Rising, turns; revealing a mask face identical with the* FIRST'S *and the* SECOND'S*)*: Overwhelmed.

DOCTOR: Well, guess we'll blow. I got some important business to attend to. Bye bye, girls.

ALL THREE FIGURES *(In unison)*: Goodbye doctor adieu Marquis. *(Turning, they resume their rocking chairs and knitting. Exeunt* DOCTOR *and* HIM.*)*

SECOND FIGURE: How often do you change the water?

FIRST: I only change it once a day but Mrs. Strong changes it twice a week.

THIRD: Has Mrs. Strong a hippopotamus?

FIRST: Two, my dear. That's where I got mine—they had kittens last May.

THIRD: I wish I'd known.

SECOND: I should have made my husband steal one for me.

FIRST: What a pity. She didn't know what to do with the other six, so she gave them to a circus.

SECOND: They're darling when they're young, aren't they?

FIRST: Perfectly darling. *(The* DOCTOR'S *head reappears in the picture. The* WOMAN'S *eyes continue closed.)*

THIRD: But I suppose it's a nuisance until the little things become housebroken.

FIRST: O you get used to that.

## Scene II

SCENE: *A room: three visible walls and an invisible wall. Of the visible walls one, the wall to the audience's left, is solid. In the middle wall is a door and in the wall to the audience's right a window.*

*Against the solid wall is a sofa on which lies a man's brown felt hat, much the worse for wear. Under the window in the opposite wall is a table on which reposes a large box for cigarettes; and near the table are two chairs in the less comfortable of which* HIM *sits, back to the audience, writing in a notebook.*

ME *(whose head appeared in the picture, preceding scene) stands facing the audience just inside the invisible fourth wall. Her open eyes (which are focussed at a point only a few inches distant) and her gestures (arranging hair, smoothing eyebrows, etc.) as well as the pose of her body (which bends slightly forward from the hips) suggest to the audience that she is looking at her reflection in an invisible mirror which hangs on this invisible wall.*

ME *(To herself)*: I look like the devil.

HIM *(Absently, without looking up or turning)*: Wanted: death's brother.

ME *(Still primping)*: No but did you ever try to go to sleep, and not be able to, and lie watching the dark and thinking about things.... *(She cocks her head, surveying herself anew. Satisfied, turns; goes to the table and stands, looking down at* HIM.*)*

HIM *(As before)*: Did I which?

ME: Nothing.

HIM *(Looks up, smiles)*: Impossible.

ME *(Touching his shoulder)*: Look. You be nice to me—you can do THAT any time.

HIM: Can I? *(Pockets notebook and pencil. Gets up, faces her.)*

ME: It's true.

HIM: What's "it"?

ME: "It" is, that you really don't care about....

HIM: I'll bite the rubber angleworm: what don't I really care about?

ME *(Sinks into the more comfortable chair)*: Anything.

HIM: Whereas this is what's untrue—. *(Sits on the table)* Anything everything nothing and something were looking for eels in a tree, when along came sleep pushing a wheelbarrow full of green mice.

ME *(To herself)*: I thought so. . . .

HIM: I, however, thought that it was the taller of the two umbrellas who lit a match when they found themselves in the main street of Hocuspocus side by each riding elephants made out of candy.

ME: And you may find this sort of thing funny. But I don't.

HIM: May I?

ME: O—suddenly I think I'd like to die.

HIM: I think myself that there's some thinking being done around here. But why die now? The morn's on the thorn, the snail's on the wing, the play's on the way; and who knows?

ME: I do. I know we're absolutely different. I've tried and tried not to know it, but what in the world is the use of trying? O, I'm so sick of trying—

HIM: Me too. This business of writing a play, I mean.

ME: You mean I'm no good to you and that we should have ended everything long ago; because—not being interested in all the ideas you're interested in—it's obviously silly of me to pretend.

HIM: To pretend? *(Picking up the box, opens it and proffers cigarettes; her hand automatically takes one. Striking a match, he lights her cigarette and his. He gets off the table; walks up and down, smoking.)* What's obviously silly of you to pretend is, that we are not in love—

ME: In love!

HIM: Precisely; otherwise we couldn't fight each other so.

ME: This may be your idea of being in love: it isn't mine. *(She smokes wearily. Pause.)*

HIM *(Halts, facing the window)*: What did you say. . . .

ME: I said, it's not my idea of love.

HIM: No; I mean when I was sitting, and you—

ME: Who cares.

HIM: —you asked me something. I have it: you couldn't go to sleep. *(Walks to the table and stands, looking down at her. After a moment, stooping, he kisses her hand.)* I'm very sorry. *(Puts his arm around her)*

ME: Stop please; I don't want you to be nice to me.

HIM: But I can't help being nice to you, because I'm in love with you. *(She shakes her head slowly)* O yes I am. You may not be in love with me, but that doesn't prevent me from being in love with you.

ME: I don't know, really. . . . O, I wish—

HIM *(Releases her)*: What?

ME: —because with part of you I think I'm in love. What can I do?

HIM: Well now let's see . . . here's a bright idea: you can advertise in the Paris edition of the New York Herald for a new lover, thus—"By a freckled fragile petite brunette incapable of loneliness and cooking, wanted: a tall strong handsome blond capable of indigestion and death (signed) Cinderella Van Winkle."

ME *(Involuntarily)*: Who's she?

HIM: Don't tell me you never in your whole life heard of Cinderella Van Winkle! The bluest blood in all Gotham my dear, directly descended from the three wise men who went to sea in a thundermug, and great-great-great-GREAT-granddaughter (twice removed) of the original and only founder of the illustrious Van Winkle family, Neverrip Van Winkle, who married a Holeproof.

ME: Being funny doesn't help.

HIM: Neither, he inadvertently answered, does being tragic.

ME: Who's being tragic?

HIM: I give it up.

ME: You mean me? I'm not being tragic, I'm being serious; because I want to decide something. I think you might help me instead of making fun of me.

HIM *(Amorously)*: There's nothing I'd rather do, my dear, than help you—

ME *(Quickly)*: I don't mean—.

HIM *(Cheerfully)*: In that case, I have a definite hunch. *(ME starts)* What in the world. . . .

ME: Yes?

HIM: What's the matter?

ME *(Confused)*: Nothing. Go on, please; I'm listening.

HIM *(Smiles)*: You're also stopping and looking, which puzzles me because I don't see the engine.

ME *(Smiling)*: There isn't any—go on. I was thinking.

HIM: And may I ask what you were thinking?

ME *(Hesitantly)*: Yes.

HIM: Well?

ME: I was thinking, when you said that . . .

HIM: When I said?

ME: —about having a hunch . . .

HIM *(Sits on the arm of her chair)*: Yes? *(His hand caresses her hair)*

ME: —about . . . a hunchback. That's all.

HIM: What about a hunchback?

ME: Nothing. They're good luck. Please tell me now; that is, if you'd like to.

HIM: "Tell" you?

ME: About the play. Do you think it'll be finished soon?

HIM: On the contrary—that is, yes. I think it will be torn up.

ME: Torn up! Why?

HIM: No good.

ME *(Earnestly)*: I'm sure it's good.

HIM: You haven't had the misfortune to read it.

ME: I'd like to—if you don't mind: can I?

HIM: Of course, if you wish. I tell you: it's no good.

ME: I'd like to read it, anyway. Have you got it in your hump?

HIM *(Jumps)*: What?

ME: —Pocket, I meant.

HIM: My God, have I a hump? *(Rising)*: Here, let me look. *(Starts toward the invisible mirror)*

ME *(Hugging him)*: Please don't be angry with me: I know I'm stupid. I can't help it.

HIM *(Laughs)*: I was just on the point of—

ME: Sh.

HIM: —of letting our mirror decide the question. *(Nods in the direction of the audience)*

ME: Were you, now? I guess men are vain—but that big mirror's no good and never was any. . . .

HIM: Like my play.

ME: Nonsense. If you really want to see yourself, I've got a little one in my—O no, I lost it.

HIM: A little one in your which?

ME: A little mirror, stupid, in my bag. I must have dropped it in a snowdrift.

HIM: Not the bag?

ME: No, the mirror. I can't find it anywhere.

HIM: Never mind: I've decided that it's safer to take your word for my looks.

ME: How sweet of you. Maybe you'll let me see the play, too? Please!

HIM: I haven't the play with me today, unfortunately.

ME: I thought you always carried notes or something around with you. *(Suspiciously)* What were you writing a moment ago?

HIM: A mere trifle, as it were. A little embonpoint to the dearly beloved master of my old prepschool at Stoneacre Heights, regretting that the undersigned is unable for pressing reasons to be present at the annual grand ball and entertainment to be held forthwith on the thirteenth Friday of next Thursday beginning with last Saturday until further notice to be furnished by—

ME *(Mystified)*: What "master"?

HIM: I doubt if you ever heard of the fellow: his name is Bates. Haha. Let us now turn to serious subjects. Assuming a zygote to result from the fusion of two gametes, the company will next attempt to visualise, through halfshut optics, a semifluid semitransparent colourless substance consisting of oxygen hydrogen carbon and nitrogen—

ME *(Smiles)*:—were looking for eels in a tree.

HIM: Precisely; when who should come along but little Mr. Mendel, wheeling a numerical law full of recurring inherited characteristics all wrong side up with their eyes shut on a slackwire tightrope. *(Vehemently)* Damn everything but the circus! *(To himself)* And here am I, patiently squeezing fourdimensional ideas into a twodimensional stage, when all of me that's anyone or anything is in the top of a circustent. . . . *(A pause)*

ME: I didn't imagine you were leading a double life—and right under my nose, too.

HIM *(Unhearing, proceeds contemptuously)*: The average "painter" "sculptor" "poet" "composer" "playwright" is a person who cannot leap through a hoop from the back of a galloping horse, make people laugh with a clown's mouth, orchestrate twenty lions.

ME: Indeed.

HIM *(To her)*: But imagine a human being who balances three chairs, one on top of another, on a wire, eighty feet in air with no net underneath, and then climbs into the top chair, sits down, and begins to swing. . . .

ME *(Shudders)*: I'm glad I never saw that—makes me dizzy just to think of it.

HIM *(Quietly)*: I never saw that either.

ME: Because nobody can do it.

HIM: Because I am that. But in another way, it's all I ever see.

ME: What is?

HIM *(Pacing up and down)*: This: I feel only one thing, I have only one conviction; it sits on three chairs in Heaven. Sometimes I look at it, with terror: it is such a perfect acrobat! The three chairs are three facts—it will quickly kick them out from under itself and will stand on air; and in that moment (because everyone will be disappointed) everyone will applaud. Meanwhile, some thousands of miles over everyone's head, over a billion empty faces, it rocks carefully and smilingly on three things, on three facts, on: I am an Artist, I am a Man, I am a Failure—it rocks and it swings and it smiles and it does not collapse tumble or die because it pays no attention to anything except itself. *(Passionately)* I feel, I am aware—every minute, every instant, I watch this trick, I am this trick, I sway—selfish and smiling and careful—above all the people. *(To himself)* And always I am repeating a simple and dark and little formula . . . always myself mutters and remutters a trivial colourless microscopic idiom—I breathe, and I swing; and I whisper: "An artist, a man, a failure, MUST PROCEED."

ME *(Timidly, after a short pause)*: This thing or person who is you, who does not pay any attention to anyone else, it will stand on air?

HIM: On air. Above the faces, lives, screams—suddenly. Easily: alone.

ME: How about the chairs?

HIM: The chairs will all fall by themselves down from the wire and be caught by anybody, by nobody; by somebody whom I don't see and who doesn't see me: perhaps by everybody.

ME: Maybe yourself—you, away up ever so high—will hear me applaud?

HIM *(Looking straight at her, smiles seriously)*: I shall see your eyes. I shall hear your heart move.

ME: Because I shall not be disappointed, like the others.

HIM: Women generally prefer the theatre, however.

ME: Women can't help liking the theatre any more than women can help liking men.

HIM: I don't understand.

ME: What I mean is perfectly simple. I mean, women like to pretend.

HIM *(Laughs gaily)*: Upon which words, our knock-kneed flybitten hero executed a spontaneous inverted quintuple backsomersault, missing the nonexistent trapeze by six and seven-eighths inches.

ME *(Looking away)*: I'm sorry—you see it's no use trying to tell me things, because I don't understand. And I can't argue.

HIM *(Walking over to her, takes her hand in his; caresses it gently)*: Wrong, wrong. *(Tries to look in her eyes which, drooping, evade his)* Please don't mistake him; it was meant as a compliment, he's a harmless acrobat, he was trying to show you that he feels how much finer you are than he is or has been or ever will be— you should pity him. *(Stroking)* Poor clown.

ME *(Withdraws her hand)*: You shouldn't play up to me.

HIM: You should know better than to accuse me of playing up to you.

ME *(In disgust)*: O, you can't know anything about men; they're so complicated.

HIM: MEN complicated!

ME: Women don't want so many things.

HIM: any woman?

ME: If she's really a woman.

HIM: What does the woman who's really a woman wish?

ME *(Looking at him)*: That's a secret.

HIM: Really?

ME: Really a secret.

HIM: A secret is something to be guessed, isn't it?

ME *(Defiantly)*: You'll never guess mine.

HIM: Perhaps, but why insult—

ME: Nobody's insulting you. I simply feel that I'm this way and there's no use in my trying to be another way.

HIM *(Smiles)*: Speaking of secrets, here's one which I've never breathed to a single soul; sabe usted quién soy?

ME: No. Do you?

HIM: Mr. Bang, the hunter. *(His voice shrinks to a whisper; he gestures mysteriously)* I hunt the gentle macrocosm with bullets made of microcosm and vice versa. *(Laughs. Suddenly serious, resumes.)* Yessiree—and this is a positively dead secret: I very frequently tell this to absolutely noone—. *(With entire earnestness, leaning importantly toward her, enunciates distinctly and cautiously)* My gun is made of chewinggum.

ME *(Quietly)*: I wish I had a piece. *(She struts the back of one doll-like hand across her forehead. Speaks vaguely.)* Where are we? I mean, who are we; what am I doing—here?

HIM: We are married.

ME: Why do you say that?

HIM: Isn't that the way married people are supposed to feel? *(Abruptly turning, walks briskly across the room; halts: half-turns, looks toward the window and mutters)* It's snowing . . . *(His voice thinks to itself)* . . . showing . . . *(His whisper marvels, muses)* . . . knowing. *(He stands, lost in thought)*

ME *(With an effort)*: Promise something.

HIM *(Absently)*: Yes?

ME: Promise that when the circus comes this year you'll take me.

HIM *(To her)*: On one condition; that you agree to see everything.

ME: Of course.

HIM: Last year you refused to pay your respects to The Queer Folk.

ME: O. *(Quickly)* But that's not the circus. And besides, whoever wants to see a lot of motheaten freaks?

HIM: I did. *(Smiles to himself)* I seem to remember riding out of a circus once upon a time on somebody's shoulder; and hearing a throbbing noise, and then a coarse voice squirting a stream of bright words—and looking, and seeing a small tent with huge pictures of all sorts of queer things, and the barker spieling like a fiend, and people all about him gaping like fish. Whereupon, I began to tremble—

ME (*Starting, as a drum sounds faintly*): Whatever's that?

HIM: —and begged somebody to take me in; which somebody probably did, I don't remember . . .

ME: I hear something, don't you? (*The noise nears*) That. It's ever so near now. Must be a parade, and on such a wintry day, too. Imagine.

HIM (*Listening vainly*): What you hear and I don't must be either an exelevated-engineer in a silk stovepipe with a sprig of shamrock in his buttonhole riding a red white and blue tricycle like mad up 5th Avenue and waving a little green flag, or Einstein receiving the keys of the city of Coral Gables in a gondola—

ME: I'm sure it's a parade!

HIM: —or a social revolution—

ME: Will you do something?

HIM: Say it with flowers. (*The noise stops*) What?

ME (*Listening*): It seems to have stopped, very near—please run out and see; will you? (HIM *stares, mildly astonished, as* ME *jumps up from the more comfortable chair and hurries to the sofa*) Here's your hat: and look, it's snowing; you'd better take—

HIM: To Hell with the umbrella. (*Takes his crumpled hat from her*) Now in just what does your most humble and very obedient servant's mission consist?

ME: You're to take a look around the corner. Because I'm almost sure there's something.

HIM: Pardon me, Your Excellency, for remarking that I think you're crazy. (*Going, he kisses her*)

ME: You don't need to tell me: I know I am. (HIM *exits through door in middle wall.* ME *walks nervously up and down—pauses: goes to the invisible mirror and stands, stares, gestures, exactly as at the beginning of the scene.)*

## Scene III

SCENE: *The picture, as at the end of Scene I (both heads present:* WOM-AN'S *eyes closed) and the three knitting rocking* FIGURES *facing the picture with their backs to the audience.*

THIRD FIGURE: I suppose so—what did you say yours was called?

FIRST: It's Toasted, but it died.

THIRD: How terrible. Did it swallow something?

FIRST: No, it fell down stairs.

SECOND: I can sympathise with you, my dear. All my children were killed in the great war.

FIRST: That's perfectly marvelous! How many did you have?

SECOND: At one time I had over eighty boys.

THIRD: Boys are the naughtiest little creatures—didn't you find them a bother?

SECOND: Not a bit, I used to keep mine out on the fire escape.

FIRST: Male or female?

SECOND: Female, so my husband says. *(Enter* HIM. *The three* FIG-URES *stop rocking and knitting.)*

HIM *(Bowing and removing his battered hat)*: I beg your pardon—. *(All three* FIGURES *rise and turn.* HIM *surveys their identical mask-faces doubtfully.)* I . . . how do you do—? *(Extends his hand to the* FIRST FIGURE, *who extends hers but instead of shaking hands twists his palm upward and studies it)*

FIRST FIGURE *(Rapidly)*: Yes Willie will.

HIM *(Confused)*: Willie—

FIRST FIGURE: Will die.

HIM *(Uncomprehending)*: Die?

FIRST FIGURE: One hour before midnight Daylight Saving Time February 30th.

HIM: —How?

FIRST FIGURE: At seventy kilometres an hour. Of ennui with complications. In a toilet of the train de luxe going from Fiesole to Fiesole. Next! *(She whisks his hand toward the* SECOND FIGURE *who takes it and studies it)*

SECOND FIGURE *(More rapidly than the* FIRST*)*: The key to the philosophy of Locke is John. Be careful not to swallow too much broken glass during the week and when riding a bicycle from or to work never take your feet off the handlebars even if a policeman smiles at traffic. Your favorite planet is Ringling Brothers. Horseradish will not produce consequences unless cowslips which is unlikely so be not daunted tho' affairs go badly since all will be well. The cards say and the tea leaves admit that enough is as good as a feast which will cause you some flatulence which you will not mind as long as Gipsy continues to remain a diurnal wateringpot but beware of a woman called Metope who is in the pay of Triglyph disguised as either an insurance agent or I forget which it doesn't matter and whenever a stuffed platitude hits you in the exaggerated omphalos respond with a threefisted aphorism to the precise casazza. Faretheewell n'erdoweel.— Next! *(She whisks his hand toward the* THIRD FIGURE, *who takes it and studies it)*

THIRD FIGURE *(More rapidly than the* SECOND*)*: You suffer from noble-blood-poisoning. Time is the autobiography of space. Give a woman everything and she has nothing. Life is a matter of being born. Treat a man like dirt and he will produce flowers. Art is a question of being alive.—Go in peace. *(She drops his hand.* HIM *crams his hat on his head and hurries out, as the* THREE FIGURES *turn sit rock and knit.)*

## Scene IV

SCENE: *The room of Scene 2 revolved clockwise with reference to the audience so that the fourth or invisible wall is now the window wall. The wall to the audience's right (corresponding to the window wall of Scene 2) is the door wall. The middle wall (corresponding to the door wall of Scene 2) is the solid wall, against which is the sofa. To the audience's left a new wall with a large mirror (the invisible fourth wall of Scene 2) is now visible.*

*ME is standing and gesturing before the mirror, as at the beginning and end of Scene 2; but at the point on the stage where she then stood there is now the table, near which are the two chairs.*

HIM *(Coming through the doorway skims his hat at the sofa)*: There wasn't anything. *(Brushes snow off himself, stamps, goes to the table: sits in the less comfortable of the chairs and pulls a notebook from his pocket)*

ME *(At the mirror speaks dimly)*: I thought there might be. *(A pause)* I was thinking. . . .

HIM *(Absently: turning leaves of notebook)*: So am I.

ME *(At the mirror)*: You could make ever so much money, if you wanted to.

HIM *(As before)*: Hm.

ME: Writing things . . . things people want—the public. Things people would like.

HIM *(Pulling out a pencil begins writing in notebook)*: Uh-huh.

ME *(Vaguely)*: Like plays and scenarios.

HIM *(Softly)*: Keyring Comedies and Keyhole Farces.

ME: Not funny necessarily.

HIM *(Parenthetically)*: Just dull.

ME: People like serious things.

HIM *(Almost inaudibly)*: The Four Horses of the Apocalypse.

ME *(Still primping)*: Because, really, you're ever so clever . . . I know that.

HIM *(Murmurs)*: You made me what I am today I hope you're satisfied.

ME: No but take—

HIM *(Starting up)*: Aha! I see it all now: The Great American Novel (gimme a chord, professor) where for the first and only time is revealed in all its startling circularity the longlost nombril of the Middle West. *(As if quoting)* Lucy T. Wot felt That Something which is nothing like anything, and as quick as everything laying her red hot pail of blackberries down in the midafternoon moonlight, slowly raised two eyes, in both after each of which a single tear strove as it were for the mastery, to those of Henery Pudd who merely looked at her however.

ME: O well. You don't want to be serious.

HIM: Serious?—I serious? You're jesting. *(Resumes writing)*

ME: I was trying to help you. *(A pause)*

HIM *(Reads to himself in a low voice)*: "If we are dolls, It pulls the strings. If we pull strings, It is the dolls: who move." *(Emerging from his thought, finds her standing beside him)*: You look terribly.

ME *(Breaking down)*: I can't help it and I've tried so hard not to talk about it and I'm sick with worrying—. *(Wrings her hands)*

HIM *(Rises: drawing her into the more comfortable chair, puts his arm over her sobbing body)*: Your hair is beautiful, today.

ME: Yes I tried that first. And I even went to the dentist—but nothing works.

HIM: Since when?

ME *(Shudders)*: O god I don't know. And I walked miles and miles till I had to sit down in the snow or any old place: I'm sorry. *(She dabs her eyes with a microscopic handkerchief)* I know I'm silly to be this way . . . I'll stop crying—really, I will. Don't be angry with me.

HIM: "Angry"?

ME: I knew you were busy and wanted to get that damned play or whatever it is done. I promised myself I wouldn't go near you or bother you. And then—I don't know . . . I couldn't. (*Chokes on a sob*) O well: now I'll stop crying.

HIM (*Muses*): "Angry"?

ME: Really I'll stop.

HIM (*Smiling*): Our artist's conception—

ME: O, You and your "artist's conception"—. (*Brushing away his arm, rises; smiles wryly*): I'm going to lie down—please go on working. (*He stares straight before him. She takes his face in her hands.*) Look at me: I'm sorry to have been so stupid. . . . (*Kisses him lightly. Goes upstage to the sofa and lies down with her back toward him and the audience.*) This is much better—I think I can go to sleep . . . good night.

HIM (*Stands for a few moments looking out the invisible window, then turns. Walks quietly to the mirror. Speaks in an almost whisper, staring at his reflection.*): If it were the first time. (*Staring always into the mirror, he passes a limp longish hand over face forehead hair*) Where's the moment—come: for an incipient dramatist you're an unearthly blockhead. You maul the climaxes always. I'll say that as a slack wire artist you're a heavenly plumber— you and your chairs! (*Laughs silently*) "Angry"?—On the contrary, better put everything in working order. Poor old flivver. She coughs, she's running on one. Dirty sparkplugs. If it were the fifteenth time, or time itself for that matter . . . Time and Space, a softshoe turn. The wellknown writer of scenarios, properties one million lemon pies, hero a spitball artist of the first water, much furniture everywhere broken, pity and terror incorporated, it all comes out in the wash, happy ending, I've got the machine who's got the god? (*Takes a step forward*) Once again for luck, let's rehearse. Ars longa vita brevis. The Est—? (*Feels of his right jacket pocket*)—Yes. Are you with me? (*Stares fixedly)* You are. Good. Now I straighten up, looking my prettiest as it were. Head, so: eyes wide open.—In a lopsided way you really are almost handsome. We look straight ahead and we move my careful hand, slowly, down along my jacket; to his pocket. I, slowly, put his hand into my pocket; easily, don't you know? Or as if looking for the thirteenth volume of the Encyclopaedia Britannica. Very good: excellent.—I should like to see myself do this. I do this very well, really. Mistaken vocation: should have been an actor perhaps?—And we take our hand out of this pocket; very slowly, so as not to. *(Withdraws his hand, with an automatic)* Perfect. That's the gesture—not quite slow enough, perhaps; otherwise. . . . And lifting our, my, his, arm, in a slow easy curve, like this; to the right temple: I do not shut my eyes. *(Stares, pistol at head. Speaks to his reflection.)* Why I'm a fool, I can never get my revenge on You. If I shut my eyes I'm not killing You. *(Bitterly)* And if I don't, it's You who kill your miserable self—quelle blague! *(His hand, with the automatic, wavers.* ME *screams. Wheeling,* HIM *pockets the pistol and bows to her.)* Morgen.

ME: —What—

HIM: It's my play: the wily villain, trapped by armies of unalterable law and so forth, commits harrycarissima with an atomizer— ought to be a howling success, don't you think? The Jarvanese way, you know. Sorry to frighten—

ME: —what's—

HIM: Would you care to inspect? *(He advances toward her. She cringes.)* Pistil. The female organ of a flower. But I only got a D plus in cryptogamic botany, when Professor Roland Thaxter was arrested for riding his bicycle on the sidewalk. *(He reaches the couch. She covers her face with her hands, speechless, cowering.)* Look. It's really very neat: in three parts, ovary style and stigma. *(He removes the magazine)* Not loaded. Don't be afraid.

ME *(Peeping between her fingers)*: I—thought. . . .

HIM: Stamen is what you thought, it contains the pollen. *(Inserts the magazine)* Hence stamina.—Are you still unhappy?

ME *(After a short pause, touching him timidly)*: Listen: did you—

HIM: You don't look unhappy. *(Slowly goes to the table, on the centre of which he carefully lays the automatic)*

ME: Did you do this—for me?

HIM: This?—I don't get you. Sorry.

ME: Because . . . I think. *(Relaxing utterly, spreads herself over the sofa—halfshut eyes smiling at the ceiling, to which she whispers)* Yes.

HIM *(Half turning, looks at her; expressionless)*: Ah. *(Opens the box, takes a cigarette and speaks, tapping the cigarette on his hand)* How is it with you, lady?

ME *(Quietly, to the ceiling)*: It's wonderful with me.

HIM *(Lights his cigarette. Sitting on the table, back to the audience, murmurs vaguely.)*: The king's to blame. Congratulations.

ME *(Vaguely murmurs)*: What . . . king.

HIM: King queen and knave, King kinkajou with his prehensile tail, King C. Y. Didn't Gillette Meknow.

ME *(As before)*: The second sounds like a nice king. . . . *(Silence,* HIM *smokes)* Are—are you busy?

HIM *(Laughs)*: "Busy"? Not just now.

ME: Then come over here, please.

HIM: Motive?

ME: Because I'm happy and I want you here. *(He strolls upstage to the couch. She makes room for him. As he sits down, she puts her arm around his neck.)* I guess I'll write a play myself—all about policemen and shootings and mirrors.

HIM: Why not.

ME: I guess my play will have ever so many more scary scenes than yours . . . nobody'll go to see your play because it won't be half so exciting. *(She laughs)* O—and mine will have something yours hasn't got: and all the mothers will bring their children to see him.

HIM: Him?

ME: The elephant.

HIM: Indeed.

ME: I'll have a fullsized elephant in my play.

HIM: With a trunk and everything?

ME: Of course. *(She looks at him for a moment: hugs him suddenly)* O you darling. With its baby face—. *(Sees his hat on the floor near the sofa)* That hat's all motheaten or something: you must buy yourself a new one. *(Hugging him, whispers)* My lover.

HIM *(After a short pause)*: What did you say then?

ME: "My lover." I can say that if I like, because it's true.

HIM *(Gently)*: Can you?—Here's something queer: I can say "that's not my hat." *(Earnestly)* And it's true.

ME: Is it, now: you mean you've given that dreadful old hat away to somebody? Not to me, I hope?

HIM *(Very gently)*: How could I give it away when it doesn't belong to me?

ME: You mean it's just a horrid old hat you've rented—by the year, I suppose

HIM: Not rented. Borrowed.

ME: Well now, that's interesting: the dirty old thing—it belongs to somebody else, you mean?

HIM: It belongs . . . to a friend of ours.

ME: Of ours? That nasty old crooked disagreeable hat?

HIM: It's the Other Man's hat.

ME: What?

HIM *(Gestures)*: Just as these are his clothes: didn't I tell you? *(Laughs)* But you knew, really. Really, you were just pretending.

ME: I knew?

HIM:—About these neckties and socks and things. *(Serious)* He lets me wear them because it amuses him.

ME: What are you talking about?

HIM: Am I?

ME: I don't understand. What other man—where?

HIM: Here, of course.

ME: Really dear, you might be serious. You know I don't understand you when you're joking.

HIM: Seriously dear, I don't wish to alarm you. But there are really two men in this room—

ME: Two—?

HIM: —one of whom is jealous of the other.

ME: Are you trying to be funny or something?

HIM: I am not trying to be funny. Seriously.

ME: O; I thought you were. What are you doing?

HIM *(mysteriously)*: Something extraordinarily dangerous. I am really sitting in this Other Man's cage and I am really being caressed by this Other Man's canary.

ME: Who is that?

HIM *(Looking at her)*: You are.

ME: "Canary"—of whom?

HIM *(Slowly)*: Your lover is in this room.

ME: My—. . . . *(Rising)* Not any longer.

HIM: O yes he is, and I can prove it.

ME: O no. You can't.

HIM: Very easily. By showing him to you. Would you care to see him now?

ME: Now. Yes.

HIM *(Rising)*: This way, ladies and gentlemen—. *(Guides her to the mirror: stands behind her)*—See?

ME *(Puzzled)*: What?

HIM: You see him, all right: why not say hello? He's looking straight at you—after all, it's no good pretending to me at that you don't know this gentleman.

ME: O. Him.

HIM: Yes; therefore—. *(Dropping suddenly on his knees, face to the mirror)*—Let us pray. *(Shuts his eyes and joins his hands)* O Mr. Man, if sometimes I seem to be taking your place, please don't be angry with me. You know perfectly well that I never seriously compete with you, Mr. Mirror Man, and I know perfectly well that you've got much too much sense to believe what the neighbors say about her and me. Not that she'd be to blame if there were anything really between us; but as a matter of fact I'm innocent, too: O Man in the Mirror, I swear I'm innocent! And since we know it's all a joke, let's speak seriously: now as for this here young woman, I know that she's always been true to you, and everybody knows; and, if you stop to think, you yourself know that you're the only fellow she's ever seriously been really in love with, or really ever seriously wanted, or seriously really ever cared about at all. *(During this speech* ME *tilts her small head sideways, inspecting herself critically; her slender hands, having pulled at dress-hips, rise to a cheek where their fingers automatically begin arranging stray wisps of hair: she stares always into the mirror.* HIM *gets up. Turns to her.)* N'est-ce pas?

ME: I'm sorry. I didn't hear what you said. *(With a final glance at herself, she strolls toward the invisible window)*

HIM *(Picking up and putting on his battered hat, smiles suddenly)*: You aren't mad, am I?

ME *(Shrugging)*: I suppose it's because I'm stupid—but somehow I don't care. . . .

HIM: Don't suppose. *(Softly)* Or if you must suppose, suppose that you are standing before a window and that continuously something happens—snow appears, covers the earth; melting, disappears—in other words, suppose that the earth rises, reappears, moves: suppose Spring. Or suppose that I am looking in a mirror and that my consciousness of the surface dissolves before an image as snow may melt before rain or as Winter melts before April and as the awake must dissolve before the asleep. . . . *(Smiles to himself)*—In other words, suppose that a part of me is talking at this moment.

ME *(Standing at the table and looking out the invisible window, speaks vaguely)*: But really, everything's winter, outside.

HIM: But seriously: the nearer something is, the more outside of me it seems. *(Walks to the sofa: pulls out notebook and reads, almost inaudibly, to himself)* "These solidities and silences which we call 'things' are not separate units of experience, but are poises, self-organising collections. There are no entities, no isolations, no abstractions; but there are departures, voyages, arrivals, contagions. I have seen an instant of consciousness as a heap of jackstraws. This heap is not inert; it is a kinesis fatally composed of countless mutually dependent stresses, a product-and-quotient of innumerable perfectly interrelated tensions. Tensions (by which any portion flowing through every other portion becomes the whole) are the technique and essence of Being: they copulate in laughter, in your least premeditated gesture are born myriads which die only to be incredibly reborn, they are eaten and drunk, we breathe and excrete them under different names. I do not stroke edges and I do not feel music but only metaphors. Metaphors are what comfort and astonish us, which are the projected brightness of ourselves—a million metaphors times or divided by a million metaphors constitute a moment or a coatsleeve—here is what we call smells and flavours, the difference between this face and another, god, never, tomorrow, love, yesterday, death or whatever yourself and myself agree to entitle that minute indestructible doll which only the artist possibly may endow with a carefully passionate gesture."

ME: . . . Maybe you mean something, I don't know.

HIM *(To noone, putting the notebook in his pocket and stretching himself wearily over the sofa)*: Ah, but don't you know that there is a further image—which appears not so much in the window of sleep as in a still deeper mirror? The planes overlap sometimes and sometimes the straight lines seem to fall. Philosophy is a dreampistol which goes off—bang—into flowers-and-candy . . . we dissolve, you and I. Stop look and listen to a fraction of myself. Life is a kind of lust which melts, producing death—a child.

ME: By the way, may I be allowed to ask a question?

HIM *(Absently)*: You may.

ME: What's all this play of yours about?

HIM *(To himself, smiling at the ceiling)*: This play of mine is all about mirrors.

ME: But who's the hero?

HIM *(To her)*: The hero of this play of mine? *(Hesitates.)* A man. . . .

ME: Naturally. What sort of a man?

HIM: The sort of a man—who is writing a play about a man who is writing a sort of a play.

ME: That's a queer hero, isn't it?

HIM: Isn't it?

ME: And what is this hero called?

HIM *(Very slowly)*: This hero is called "Mr. O.Him, the Man in the Mirror."

ME: O.Him. *(Smiles)* And the heroine? *(Quickly)*—or isn't there any?

HIM: On the contrary. My heroine lives over there—. *(Points to the mirror)*

ME *(Turning, at the invisible window)*: Me?

HIM: Me, the beautiful mistress of the extraordinary Mr. O.Him.

ME:—Extraordinary because he thinks she's beautiful?

HIM: Extraordinary because I need a shave because he needs a shave.

## Scene V

SCENE: *The picture, as in Scene 3 (both heads present:* WOMAN'S *eyes closed) and the three knitting rocking* FIGURES *facing the picture with their backs to the audience.*

SECOND FIGURE: Seesaw Margery Daw.

THIRD: Four out of five will get wedlock.

FIRST: How can I when it's Friday the 13th?

THIRD: By reading the gospel according to Saint Freud.

SECOND: Nobody would be the wiser for a glass of mercury.

FIRST: But have you ever tried standing on the third rail?

SECOND: Yes except that February has too many holidays.

FIRST: In Vino Veritas.

THIRD: Beware of pickpockets.

SECOND: Look at Napoleon: he lost the Battle of Waterloo.

THIRD: And what happened to Jesus Christ? They crucified him.

FIRST: Quite the contrary. They took after their mother.

THIRD: Immediately?

FIRST: No, with salt and pepper and of course a dash of lemon.

SECOND: But I only got beyond page six, when nothing happened and the conductor died in my lap.

FIRST: It has wings, I think.

THIRD: That's the insidious thing about hippocampus (unpleasant breath).

SECOND: Atlantic coast from Cape Cod to Charleston.

FIRST: Greatest length seven inches.

THIRD: A Pacific Coast species grows nearly twelve inches long.

SECOND: The young are carried in a pouch by the male.

THIRD: The only fish with a grasping tail.

· CURTAIN ·

# ACT TWO

## Scene I

SCENE: *That amount of the actual structure of the stage etc. which lies behind the plane of the curtain is revealed, by the curtain's rising, without a "set" of any kind.*

*The action or content of Scene I consists of the curtain's rising, of its absence for one minute and of its falling. Darkness.*

VOICE OF ME: Was that an accident? Or a scene?

VOICE OF HIM: Both I trust.

VOICE OF ME: Did it really mean something?

VOICE OF HIM: It meant nothing, or rather: death.

VOICE OF ME: O, I see.

VOICE OF HIM: This is the Other Play.

VOICE OF ME: By Mr. O.Him?

VOICE OF HIM:—The Man in the Mirror.

VOICE OF ME: But tell me, what's this Other Play all about?

VOICE OF HIM: About? It's about anything you like, about nothing and something and everything, about blood and thunder and love and death—in fact, about as much as you can stand. (I might add that it's sure of a long run; provided, of course, we receive the proper advertising—you know what I mean—"Broadway is enjoying a novel treat in one of the wittiest and most highly original products of American genius, entitled 'How Dyuh Get That Way?' By the authors of 'Nuf Ced' . . . the subject of this rollicking farce is the 18th Amendment; and right now we want to ask you, could anything be funnier? . . . but just to show how screamingly and even killingly funny 'How Dyuh Get That Way?' is, we are going to give the assembled company a sample, taken at random: the scene is a lawn with the porch of a bungalow to the audience's right, the time is the wee small hours.)"—Are you ready?

## Scene II

SCENE: *As previously described.*

*Enter staggeringly three corpulent* MIDDLE-AGED MEN, *the* THIRD *of whom is played by the* DOCTOR.

FIRST MIDDLE-AGED MAN *(Heartily)*: Jon playa gaim croquet.

SECOND *(Irritably)*: Oreye bjush wummore Ished.

THIRD *(Loftily)*: Sridiculous croquet lesh play tennish.

FIRST *(Delightedly)*: Tennish love tennish mfavorite gaim.

SECOND *(Angrily)*: Oreye bjush wummore Ished.

THIRD *(Scornfully)*: Jon ystewed.

SECOND *(Fiercely)*: Oreye bjush wummore.

FIRST *(Rapturously)*: Hoosh gota raquet.

THIRD *(Witheringly)*: Turrbly shtewed shdishgraysh.

FIRST *(Wildly)*: Hoosh gota raquet wanta play tennish.

SECOND *(Furiously)*: Wummore.

THIRD *(Annihilatingly)*: Youghta gome.

SECOND *(Savagely)*: Wummore.

THIRD *(Abolishingly)*: Gome goat bed.

FIRST *(Desperately)*: Somebody mushave raquet mush play tennish witha raquet. *(Enter from the left one spinster, or* VIRGO, *with a very red nose, clad in black pajamas and carrying a dripping candle)*

VIRGO: O you big bad old men, you extraordinarily naughty husbands, you typically depraved old things: aren't you just lovely?

SECOND MIDDLE-AGED MAN: Wummore.

THIRD *(To* FIRST*)*: Shpoleashman shudup.

FIRST: Shnot poleashman shfriend mine hullo.

VIRGO: You naughty old thing: how dare you speak to me!

FIRST MIDDLE-AGED MAN: Gota tennish raquet?

SECOND: Wummore.

THIRD: Shudup.

VIRGO: O you terribly intoxicated old reprobates, you perfectly sweet old wretches, I don't understand a word you say.

THIRD MIDDLE-AGED MAN: Officer musha pologise frien vurry drunk shdishgraysh.

SECOND: Oreye. Bjush.

FIRST *(Indicating the* VIRGO *with an ample gesture)*: Shoreye shfrien mine shgot tennish raquet.

VIRGO: O you lovely old rascals, aren't you simply ashamed of yourselves? What would your poor wives do if they could see you now!

FIRST MIDDLE-AGED MAN: Gimme tennish raquet oleman wanta play tennish. *(He takes hold of the candle)*

VIRGO: You old wretch: don't you dare touch my candle! Just you take those naughty hands away now!

THIRD MIDDLE-AGED MAN: Doan sult thoffcer Fred.

VIRGO: O the rascal—he's got it away from me! Whatever will I do: it's pitch dark, and what a position for a woman! *(Loudly)* I'm perfectly defenceless.

FIRST MIDDLE-AGED MAN: Thangsh oleman musha blige kmon Jon play tennish now gota raquet. *(He makes a pass with the candle)*

VIRGO: Should I scream?—But what good would that do? O, what wicked old men you are!

SECOND MIDDLE-AGED MAN: Oreye b-

FIRST: Kmon Jon kmon George bye oletop rully musha blige tyou kmon everybody goint play tennish. *(Exit)*

SECOND: Oreye. *(Exit)*

THIRD: Doan mine offcer sall fun promise frien bring it rye back frien vurry drunk jush fun yknow course yunnerstan see ylater oreye goobye mush blige. *(Exit)*

VIRGO *(Sola)*: Weren't they simply awful! Aren't men the dreadfulest wretches! And that old devil who took my candle away from me, wasn't he the limit—the poor dear thought it was a tennis raquet, can you imagine that! As for the other little man, who was simply unthinkably intoxicated, he could only say two or three words, poor dear! And then the one who spoke to me as if I were a policeman—rascally old darling! My, how I'd hate to be their wives!—I must go to bed at once before I catch my death of cold. *(Utters a profound sigh)* It was really lucky they were all in such a deplorable condition, otherwise I should have felt guilty of immodesty. . . . *(Sighs even more profoundly)* What a terrible thing it is to be a woman! *(Enter a negro redcap Grand Central porter)*

PORTER *(Saluting VIRGO)*: Pardon me mam but is you de party asked me to find out about checkin' a pet canary?

VIRGO *(Ecstatically)*: My name is Gloria Quackenbush I am a dancer three years ago I had so much indigestion and constipation that I got terribly run down I was too tired and nervous to take my lessons a lady recommended yeast the constipation was relieved and I had much less trouble with gas now I am strong in every way the hydroplane in the photograph was furnished by the yeast company. *(Darkness)*

VOICE OF HIM: You don't seem very enthusiastic.

VOICE OF ME: I'm not.

VOICE OF HIM: In that case, I have a bright idea. I am going to make a million dollars.

VOICE OF ME: You!

VOICE OF HIM: Sounds incredible, doesn't it?

VOICE OF ME: No but how?

VOICE OF HIM: I shall buy paste and labels and I shall buy boxes and I shall buy pen and ink and breadcrumbs and I shall put all of the breadcrumbs in all of the boxes and I shall write the word RA-DI-O-LE-UM on all of the labels and I shall paste all of the labels on all of the boxes.

VOICE OF ME: Is that all?

VOICE OF HIM: No. I shall insert, in all of the leading newspapers and periodicals of the country, a full page advertisement.

VOICE OF ME: Saying what?

VOICE OF HIM: Saying: "WHY DIE? TRY RA-DI-O-LE-UM." . . .

## Scene III

SCENE: *A streetcorner. People passing to and fro.*

*A* SOAP BOX ORATOR, *played by the* DOCTOR, *arrives and establishes himself.*

SOAP BOX ORATOR *(To an as yet nonexistent audience):* Ladies and gentlemen: do I look like the sort of fellow that goes around trying to drape the universe in deep mourning? Am I one of those lopsided pessimists that perambulate all over this beautiful world trying to persuade everybody he runs into that sunlight costs a million dollars a quart? *(Somebody stops to look and listen)* Is that the effect I make on you as I stand here today—I, that was born and raised on this very street and worked hard all of my life in this fair city for fifty-two years and enjoyed every moment of it? *(Two people stop to look and listen)* Am I a squeaking squealer or a squealing squawker or a whimpering morbid foureyed crapehanging meanderer? I see by your faces, ladies and gentlemen, that you don't believe so. *(Three people stop to look and listen)* All right. But let me tell you something. *(Four people stop to look and listen)* Every ten men and women I see, walking or talking or shopping or going to the movies or riding in taxicabs buses subways and elevateds or doing nothing whatever or minding the children or reading the newspaper or up in the air in airoplanes, I say to myself—five out of four will get cinderella and the other nine have it already. *(Five people stop to look and listen)* Now let's get right down to fundamentals: what is cinderella? I'm here to tell you, ladies and gentlemen, that cinderella is a newly discovered disease. *(Six people stop to look and listen)* You will ask me—is it dangerous?—Dangerous, ladies and gentlemen? Why it's so dangerous that, compared with the untold dangers to which cinderella subjects each and every specimen of the human race without exception in particular and mankind in general, a monthold baby cutting its milk teeth on a stick of dynamite is a picture of perfect safety.—Dangerous? Why, it's so dangerous that the three greatest elocutionists of all time—Demosthenes Daniel Webster and William Jennings Bryan—couldn't explain to you how dangerous cinderella is if they lectured steadily for six months without a glass of water.—Dangerous? Why, if I could begin to convey to your superior intelligences how dangerous this infernal and unprecedented disease known to scientists as cinderella is, I could pick strawberries in the Garden of Eden or fight the American Revolution. *(Seven people stop to look and listen)*—Is it dangerous? Gracious Heavens, ladies and gentlemen, cinderella is the darkest deepest awfulest most obscure insidious hideous and perfectly fatal malady on the face of God's footstool! *(Eight people stop to look and listen)* Now let me give you a little illustration, just to show you how incredibly dangerous cinderella is.—Suppose you've got cinderella (that most contagious of human diseases) or I've got cinderella, or the fellow over there's got cinderella: do we know we've got it? No, ladies and gentlemen, we don't know and we can't know! *(Nine people stop to look and listen)* We may be rotting internally, our lungs intestines livers and other glands both great and small may be silently putrefying, forming invisible pockets of nauseous pus, creating microscopic sacs of virulent poison—and we don't know it! We may be neat and clean and washed and manicured outside, and inside we may be noisome squirming garbage cans breeding billions upon trillions of repulsive wormlike omnivorous germs of cinderella: that's what the scientists have just discovered! Think of it. Dream of it, ladies and gentlemen! And you ask me if this frightful disease is dangerous! Once and for all, let me tell you that cinderella is not dangerous—it is Death Itself! *(Ten people stop to look and listen)* I see you're terrified, ladies and gentlemen, and I don't blame you. If you weren't afraid of death you wouldn't be human. But I'm not here primarily to give you the fright of your lives. Primarily, ladies and gentlemen, I'm here to help you. And I bring the greatest message of blessed comfort that the human soul in this day and time can possibly imagine. For—mark my words—in this little commongarden ordinary unassuming box reposes, to put it mildly, the secret of the ages. *(He holds up a tin pillbox. Nine people stop to look and listen.)* Now give me your close attention: when a forest fire starts, we fight the fire with fire, don't we? When a new demon of disease makes his infernal appearance on the face of this planet we turn for help to the latest discoveries of modern science, don't we? *(Eight people stop to look and listen)* In this case, ladies and gentlemen, we turn with confidence to that most entirely miraculous of all miracles: Radium. *(Seven people stop to look and listen)* And we find that our hopes are not unfounded. A new light breaks upon us—Radium will conquer cinderella! We are saved! Mankind, the whole human race, is saved! *(Six people stop to look and listen)* Step right up, ladies and gentlemen. Feast your minds upon the unimaginable treasure which this little innocentlooking box represents and contains. Try to picture to yourself the inherent wonderfulness of its mysterious contents. Think, or try to think, that the medicine comprised in each of the twelve tiny threedimensional oblate spheroids herein uselessly reposing is powerful enough to obliterate annihilate and utterly incinerate five hundred quadrillion cinderella bacteria! *(Five people stop to look and listen)* All over the universe, ladies and gentlemen, myriads of yearning hands without exaggeration are hopelessly reaching for the secret of life enclosed in this negligible bit of metal. Tomorrow in this very city a hundred hearts will breathe paeons of thankfulness for the salvation that has come to them through this tiniest receptacle. And why? Because in this modest pillbox, ladies and gentlemen, cinderella—the dreaded cinderella—meets its doom! *(Four people stop to look and listen)*—Ah, if the handful of thankful hearts that will have sampled the delicioustasting automatically assimilated contents of this little box by tomorrow morning could only be a thousand—a million—a decillion! *(Three people stop to look and listen)* But the remedy is limited, ladies and gentlemen. So infinitely precious and prophylactic a product could not be manufactured rapidly. In time to come we hope to be able to place this miracle on the market in large quantities. With this end in view and no other, our fourteen model factories at Kankakee Illinois are working night and day. We will do our best, but we too are only human. The effort involved is inconceivable. As for the expense, it is simply without exaggeration fabulous. *(Two people stop to look and listen)* But we don't trouble ourselves on that account: we are not here to make money, but to save our fellowmen and fellowwomen and fellowchildren from the most vomitory fate that has ever threatened humanity in the world's entire history. *(One person stops to look and listen)* As a conclusive proof of what I say, let me mention that we are offering the first batch of our absolutely unique and positively guaranteed product at a dead loss—we are in fact giving it away for less than the cost of printing the labels. Ladies and gentlemen, although my statements hitherto may have seemed unbelievable I have one yet to make which for sheer unadulterated unbelievability outdoes them all—the actual expense to each and every purchaser of this lifegiving panacea, is today here and now in this greatest and most prosperous of cities New York, one dollar. *(Nineteen people go their nineteen ways)* Here you are: one dollar. *(Seventeen people go their seventeen ways)* Think of it! *(Fifteen people go their fifteen ways)* Why the heavily silverplated highlypolished universally useful fully guaranteed aluminium box alone is worth a dollar. *(Thirteen people go their thirteen ways)* It lasts a lifetime! *(Eleven people go their eleven ways)* Squeeze drop shake it you can't break it, feed it to the lions roll it over Niagara Falls shoot burn and sit down on it it's indestructible turn and twist it at your will if it breaks we pay the bill round and over inside forward wrongside downside upside out—ladies and gentlemen, it remains one and the same. *(Nine people go their nine ways)* Step right up! *(Seven people go their seven ways)* Each and every package positively guaranteed to contain authentic infinitesimal amounts of the world's most precious substance Radium, one cubic ounce of which according to painstakingly prepared strictly scientific statistics would generate sufficient dynamic energy to instigate a crop of beautiful lovely luxuriant curly chestnut hair slightly more than five miles long all over the entire surface of the terrestrial globe in six and seven-eighths seconds. *(Five people go their five ways)* Step right up—here you are! *(Three people go their three ways, leaving only the original somebody who stopped to look and listen)* You may not have cinderella but if you haven't it's a cinch you've got something else and no matter what it is this little box will save your life one dose alone irrevocably guaranteed to instantaneously eliminate permanently prevent and otherwise completely cure toothache sleeplessness clubfeet mumps stuttering varicose veins youthful errors tonsilitis rheumatism lockjaw pyorrhea stomachache hernia tuberculosis nervous debility impotence halitosis and falling down stairs or your money back. *(The original somebody goes his original way. Darkness.)*

VOICE OF ME: That wasn't such a bright idea after all.

VOICE OF HIM: Never mind. I have another.

VOICE OF ME: Another bright idea?

VOICE OF HIM: Posolutely absitively.

VOICE OF ME: May I hear it?

VOICE OF HIM: You may. . . .

VOICE OF ME: Well?

VOICE OF HIM: . . . Well—next we have, ladies and gentlemen, Will and Bill: two partners in business who, through association, became each other. Camera!

## Scene IV

SCENE: *An inner office.*

> *At a desk is seated* WILL, *a figure with a mask face which represents the real face of the* DOCTOR, *who presently enters, playing the part of an* INTRUDER.

WILL *(Looking up, starts: gasps)*: Who are you?

INTRUDER: You mean "Who am I."

WILL *(In a shaky voice)*: Certainly: that's what I said.

INTRUDER: No. That's what I said.

WILL: Is that so. . . . *(His right hand, fumbling, opens a drawer in the desk)* . . . And what did I say?

38

INTRUDER: "Who are you."

WILL *(Covers the* INTRUDER *with a pistol)*: Will you answer?

INTRUDER *(Imperturbably)*: Answer—?

WILL: Will you answer?—Yes or no?

INTRUDER: Which?

WILL: Which—what?

INTRUDER: Which question.

WILL: You know which question—come on now: who are you?

INTRUDER *(Slowly)*: I am.

WILL *(Rising, ejaculates tremulously)*: —I?

INTRUDER: You. *(A few seconds' pause)*

WILL *(Exploding in hysterical laughter, calls out)*: Hey Bill!—Come in here a minute: I got something to show you. (BILL, *a figure with a different mask face, hurries in)*

BILL: What's the matter Will?

WILL: Matter?—I ask this feller who he is and he says "You," did you ever hear anything like that?

INTRUDER: Not you—You.

BILL *(Looking about him apprehensively)*: Me?—Who? Which feller? —Where?

WILL *(To* INTRUDER*)*: Shut up, YOU.—Listen Bill, this feller comes walking through the door like he owned the place or something.

BILL *(Catching sight of the pistol)*: What the—. Will! For Christ's sake, drop that gun—

WILL: Drop nothing. With this feller here, refusing to answer who he is? Are you crazy?

BILL: Where? What feller?—Be careful, Will, it's loaded—it might go off—

WILL: I'll shoot the sonofabitch if he don't answer me: answer, YOU—who are you?

BILL: —Will for God's sake—. *(He covers his eyes with both hands)*

INTRUDER: You.

WILL: God damn you—. *(He pulls the trigger: there is no explosion: he falls forward, writhes on the floor and collapses, with his mask face turned to the audience)*

BILL: Will!—O god: he's killed himself . . . what'll I do—O what'll I do . . . . *(Throws himself on his knees beside the body, as Irving Berlin's "What'll I Do" is heard dimly. The* INTRUDER *stealthily passes to the desk and quietly sits where* WILL *was originally seated.)*

INTRUDER: Get the police to arrest you.

BILL *(Vaguely, staring at nothing)*: What's that . . . arrest who?

INTRUDER: You.

BILL *(As before)*: . . . Me?

INTRUDER: You.

BILL *(As before)*: What did I do. What for?

INTRUDER: For murdering Will, Bill.

BILL *(Starts violently)*: I never killed Will—

INTRUDER: Why did you kill me Bill?

BILL *(Straightening, sees the* INTRUDER *for the first time—starts—his left hand with an involuntary meaningless gesture strikes the prone* WILL'S *mask face, which comes off, revealing a real face to which the mask face of* BILL *corresponds)*

INTRUDER *(Softly)*: You shouldn't have killed me, Bill.

BILL *(To* INTRUDER *with a gasp of recognition)*: —Will!

INTRUDER: Yes Bill, it's Will.

BILL: But you . . . you can't, it ain't possible—. *(Cries out)* He's dead: look at him—. *(His voice sinks to a wondering whisper as he stares unseeingly in the direction of the prone figure)* . . . My god—. Gone! *(His gaze travels gradually back to the* INTRUDER'S *face)*

INTRUDER: I am Will and I am dead because you killed me, Bill.

BILL *(Gradually rising from his knees)*: I . . . I never . . . he killed—himself—

INTRUDER: You killed Will, Bill.

BILL: . . . So help me God—I aint lying—if I'm lying, kill me!

INTRUDER *(Sternly)*: Bill killed Will and you know it.

BILL *(Writhing in an agony of remorse: anguish sprouting in his body)*:
I'm innocent—I swear I'm innocent: kill me if I aint—

INTRUDER *(Solemnly)*: You ain't, Bill.

BILL *(With a stuttering gesture of hands outstretched against some unbelievable horror, screams suddenly)*: Will!

INTRUDER: Dead, Bill.

BILL *(Sobbing)*: Why—why did I—why did—

INTRUDER: For a woman, Bill. You killed me for a woman.

BILL *(Wrapping his maskface in shivering hands)*: O——. *(He collapses,
groveling, at the* INTRUDER'S *feet. A pause.)*

INTRUDER: Bill. *(No answer. He speaks gently.)* Come Bill.

BILL *(Upwrithing—petrified)*: O——.

INTRUDER: Come with me, now. *(Suddenly grabs* BILL, *who goes
utterly limp in his grip: shouts, in a completely changed voice)*
All right boys—I got her! *(Noise of a door being broken down.
Darkness.)*

VOICE OF HIM: May I be so indiscreet as humbly to beg your Royal
Highness's most illustrious verdict upon that deplorable scene?

VOICE OF ME: It made me feel as if I'd just swallowed a caterpillar.

VOICE OF HIM: These masks and ghosts, however, lead us into girls
and dolls.

VOICE OF ME: Masks and ghosts?

VOICE OF HIM: Larva, pupa and (if we are very lucky) imago: the
instantaneous futility.—You mentioned caterpillars, and so I
am talking about caterpillars which I consider very interesting.

VOICE OF ME: I dare say everything is interesting if you understand
it. Even angleworms are probably intensely interesting, in their
way.

VOICE OF HIM: Life is a cribhouse, darling: a cribhouse with only one
door: and when we step out of it—who knows but that angleworms are prodigiously and even unnecessarily interesting?

VOICE OF ME: And who cares?

VOICE OF HIM: Certainly not angleworms—eyeless and epicene which wander in ignorant darkness.

## Scene V

SCENE: *The stage has become a semicircular piece of depth, at whose inmost point nine black stairs lead up to a white curtain.*

*Two coalblack figures, one* MALE *and one* FEMALE, *appear at opposite extremities of the semicircle's circumference (i.e. of the foreground). The* FEMALE *figure is holding in its arms a large boydoll at whom it looks fondly.*

MALE *(Nervously)*: Who you nigga?

FEMALE *(Looking up, answers lazily)*: Ahs de ground.

MALE *(Apprehensively)*: Who de ground?

FEMALE *(Proudly)*: Ahs de ground.

MALE *(Fearfully)*: Wot, you de ground?

FEMALE *(Insolently)*: Yas ahs de ground, ahs de ripe rich deep sweet sleek an sleepy ground, de G-R-O-U-N-D GROUND. *(Strolls toward centre of semicircle)*

MALE *(Faintly, pointing to the doll)*: Wot you got dere.

FEMALE *(Strolling, speaks angrily)*: Dere? Where.

MALE *(Breathlessly)*: In yo arms.

FEMALE *(Pausing at the centre of the semicircle, speaks sullenly)*: Ah got Johnie.

MALE *(Wildly)*:—O Lawd! Johnie's in de arms of de ground! *(*SIX COALBLACK FIGURES, *three male and three female, appear in succession, punctuating the circumference of the semicircle at regular intervals and in a counterclockwise direction with reference to the audience)*

FIRST *(Appearing, speaks rapidly)*: De ground's got a hold of Johnie.

SECOND (*Appearing, speaks more rapidly*): De ground's got Johnie in her arms.

THIRD (*Appearing, speaks very rapidly*): De ground won't let go.

FOURTH (*Appearing, speaks very rapidly and shrilly*): Money won't make de ground let go.

FIFTH (*Appearing, speaks shrilly and almost incoherently*): Love won't make de ground let go.

SIXTH (*Appearing, cries hysterically*): Nothin won't make de ground let go of Johnie.

ALL SIX (*In unison, hysterically*): De ground won't let go, WON'T LET GO, WON'T LET GO! (*They rightface simultaneously and march around the* FEMALE *figure with its doll. Marching, they speak in succession.*)

FIRST:      Look at Johnie
            was a man
            love a woman
            like a man only can.

SECOND:     He loved her hands
            an he loved her lips
            an he loved her feet
            an he loved her hips.

THIRD:      He loved her eyes
            an he loved her breasts
            but he loved her something
            else the best.

FOURTH:     Now he lies
            without a sound
            lonely an small
            in de arms of de ground.

FIFTH:　　Maybe he twists
　　　　　maybe he squirms
　　　　　an maybe he's full
　　　　　of lil bright worms.

SIXTH:　　After workin an ashirkin
　　　　　eatin an adrinkin
　　　　　living an alovin
　　　　　Johnie's in de ground.

*(Behind the white curtain an invisible jazz band plays softly: the voices of the players darkly sing. The* SIX FIGURES *halt, in a circle, listening.)*

VOICES:　　Frankie and Johnie were lovers
　　　　　sweet Christ how they could love
　　　　　they swore to be true to each other
　　　　　as true as the stars above
　　　　　　　but he was a man
　　　　　　　and he done her wrong

　　　　　Frankie she lived in the cribhouse
　　　　　the cribhouse had only one door
　　　　　she gave all her money to Johnie
　　　　　who spent it on a parlorhouse whore
　　　　　　　he was a man
　　　　　　　and he done her wrong

　　　　　Frankie went down to the corner
　　　　　tu buy herself a bottle of beer
　　　　　and she said to the old bartender
　　　　　have you seen my loving Johnie in here
　　　　　　　he is a man
　　　　　　　and he done me wrong

I aint agoing to tell you no secrets
and I aint agoing to tell you no lies
but Johnie went out just a minute ago
with that old whore Fanny Fry
      he is a man
      and he done you wrong

Frankie went back to the cribhouse
this time it wasn't for fun
for under her old red kimona
she carried Johnie's .44 gun
      she was looking for the man
      who done her wrong

Frankie she went to the parlorhouse
she looked in the window so high
and there she saw her Johnie
just a————-————Fanny Fry
      he was a man
      and he done her wrong

Frankie she went to the front door
she rang the front door bell
she said stand back all you pimps and whores
or I'll blow you all to Hell
      I want my man
      who done me wrong

Frankie went into the parlor
Johnie commenced to run
she said don't run from the woman you love
or I'll shoot you with your own damn gun
      you are a man
      who done me wrong

Frankie went into the parlor
Johnie hollered Frankie don't shoot
but Frankie she out with Johnie's .44 gun
and three times rootytoottoot
    she shot her man
    who done her wrong

Roll me over gently
roll me over slow
roll me over on my right side
'cause my left side's hurting me so
    you've killed your man
    who done you wrong

Frankie she turned him on his stomach
Frankie she turned him on his side
when she turned him for the third time
he hung his head and died
    she killed her man
    who done her wrong

*(The white curtain at the top of the nine black stairs is pulled aside suddenly: the* NINE PLAYERS, *in vermillion suits, with white shirts and socks, emeraldgreen neckties, lemoncoloured gloves and silk hats, appear)*

NINE PLAYERS *(Playing, singing and descending the nine black stairs)*:
    GET OUT YOUR RUBBERTIRED CARRIAGES
    AND GET OUT YOUR DECORATED HACKS
    I'LL TAKE MY LOVING JOHNIE TO THE CEMETERY
    BUT I'LL BRING HIS—

*(A cadaverous* PERSONAGE *with tortoiseshell spectacles spouts up out of the third row of the audience)*

PERSONAGE *(Played by the* DOCTOR*)*: Stop! *(The song ceases. The* SIX COALBLACK FIGURES *slink to their original positions, as the* FEMALE *figure with its doll rushes up the nine black stairs and vanishes behind the reappearing white curtain. The* MALE *figure advances indignantly.)*

MALE: Who you.

PERSONAGE *(Displays enormous badge)*: John Rutter, President pro tem. of the Society for the Contraception of Vice. *(He points a cadaverous finger at the* MALE *figure)* You were about to utter enunciate pronounce and otherwise emit a filthy lewd indecent vile obscene lascivious disgusting word!

MALE *(In astonishment)*: O Lawd; was ah?

PERSONAGE: Don't deny it! *(He climbs over the footlights and steps up to the* MALE *figure. Producing from his inside jacket pocket a paper, he seizes the* MALE *figure's right hand and—holding the hand aloft—reads glibly from the paper.)* I John Smith nose protruding eyes open ears symmetrical being in my right mind do hereby swear to obstruct impede combat hinder prevent and otherwise by every means known and unknown including extravasation knockoutdrops hypnotism and dynamite oppose the propagation or dissemination of any immediately or ulteriorly morally noxious or injurious or in any other way whatsoever harmful titillation provocation or excitation complete or incomplete of the human or inhuman mind or body or any portion of the same under no matter what conditions or any assumption of or allusion to the existence of such a tendency in the human species whether such illusion or assumption be oral graphic neither or both and including with the written and spoken word the unwritten and unspoken word or any inscription sign or mark such as has been known to occur in public places of a strictly private character commonly or uncommonly known as comfort stations or any other visible or invisible natural or unnatural assumption of or inclination to assume such a tendency or any assumption of assumption of such tendency whether comprehensible or incomprehensible intentional or unintentional premeditated or spontaneous implicit or explicit uttered or unuttered perceptible or imperceptible or any blasphemous filthy and new idea or group of ideas such as birthcontrol bolshevism and so forth and in general anything at all whatsoever be its origin or essence both irrespective of and with reference to its nature or content such as in the opinion of a judge familiar with the more widely used symbols of the English and American alphabets may can must might could would or should constitute a tacit misdemeanor against the soul of a child of not less than one day and not more than one year old and I take this oath willingly and without mental reservation on my part of any kind whatsoever conscious unconscious or foreconscious so help me God one dollar please. *(Releases the right hand of* MALE *figure. Pockets the paper.)*

MALE *(Weakly)*: Ah ain got one dollar boss. *(The white curtain at the top of the nine black stairs is suddenly pulled aside: a slender negress in a red kimona willows down the nine black stairs, passes the* NINE PLAYERS, *arrives behind the* PERSONAGE *and bumps him with her elbow)*

NEGRESS: Gway yoh poor whytrash.

PERSONAGE *(Wheeling)*: Look here, young lady, that's no way to address—

NEGRESS: Doan call me "young lady" yoh bowlegged fish: ah ain no "young lady," thang Gawd!

PERSONAGE: In that case, I should advise you to attempt by every method practicable and impracticable to conceal the fact instead of making it glaringly apparent—

NEGRESS *(Drawing herself up proudly before him, speaks contemptuously)*: Do yoh all know who ah am? *(The* PERSONAGE *recoils)*— Ah'm Frankie!

MALE FIGURE, SIX COALBLACK FIGURES *and* NINE PLAYERS *(simultaneously)*: SHE'S FRANKIE!

NEGRESS *(To* PERSONAGE*)*: Take dat! *(Whisking into view something which suggests a banana in size and shape and which is carefully wrapped in a bloody napkin, points it straight at the* PERSONAGE—*who utters a scream, jumps over the footlights, rushes up the main aisle of the theatre and disappears.* FRANKIE *turns to the audience: cradling the Something in her arms, as the* GROUND *cradled her boydoll, she takes up the song where the* PERSONAGE *interrupted it.)*—But I'll bring his—*(The drummer taps twice)* back—

EVERYBODY *(Triumphantly)*:

> BEST PART OF THE MAN
> WHO DONE ME WRONG

*(Darkness)*

VOICE OF ME: Tell me. . . .

VOICE OF HIM WHAT? *(A silence)*: So you're getting horribly bored with the other play.

VOICE OF ME: Why should you think I was bored?

VOICE OF HIM: I can't imagine. How did you like that fifth scene?

VOICE OF ME: Let's finish up this Other Play; then I'll be able to judge much better.

VOICE OF HIM: It's not my funeral.

VOICE OF ME: What comes next?

VOICE OF HIM: But will you promise to let me know when you've had enough?

VOICE OF ME: I promise.

VOICE OF HIM: Good.—In that case, ladies and gentlemen, the next scene is all about eels in a tree.

VOICE OF ME: I hope there are no mice in it—are there?

VOICE OF HIM: Not a mice.

## Scene VI

SCENE: *Fifth Avenue—midnight.*

*A* PLAINCLOTHESMAN, *his entire being focussed on something just offstage to the audience's left, stalks this invisible something minutely. He is played by the* DOCTOR.

*Enter an* ENGLISHMAN *in evening clothes and a silk hat, staggering under a huge trunk marked* FRAGILE—*his silk hat falls off. He looks at it ruefully, even hopelessly. Then an expression of tranquility adorns his visage, as he catches sight of the* PLAINCLOTHESMAN'S *back—he clears his throat several times—having failed to attract the* PLAINCLOTHESMAN'S *attention, he exclaims "I say" and "Beg pardon" and "By the way"—finally, desperate, he wheels and gently bumps the* PLAINCLOTHESMAN *with the trunk. The* PLAINCLOTHESMAN *leaps into the air: landing with a drawn automatic, stares his innocent vis-à-vis fiercely in the eye.*

ENGLISHMAN: Ah—good evening. Excuse me. Would you mind awfully—you see, my topper just fell off.

PLAINCLOTHESMAN: Yuh wut?

ENGLISHMAN: My topper, my hat—would you be so awfully kind as to hand it to me? *(The* PLAINCLOTHESMAN *contemplates the* ENGLISHMAN *from top to toe: his jowl emits a cynical leer; pocketing his automatic, and warily stooping, he picks up the silk hat and inspects it with deep suspicion)*

ENGLISHMAN *(Cheerfully sticking out his head)*: On my nut please, if you don't mind. *(The* PLAINCLOTHESMAN *scowls ominously: places the silk hat grimly on the* ENGLISHMAN'S *head)* Glad to have met you—*(He starts for the wings, right)* Cheerio!

PLAINCLOTHESMAN: HAY. *(The* ENGLISHMAN *starts: staggers: turns)* Lissun. Wutchuhgut dare.

ENGLISHMAN (*Apprehensively, trying to look behind himself*): There? Where?

PLAINCLOTHESMAN: On yuh back uv coarse.

ENGLISHMAN (*Relieved*): O, you mean that?—(*He tries to nod at what he carries*)—Don't tell me you don't know what that is.

PLAINCLOTHESMAN: Sie. Dyuh tink I doughno uh trunk wen I sees it?

ENGLISHMAN (*Perplexed*): Trunk? I said nothing about a trunk.

PLAINCLOTHESMAN: Youse dough need tuh. Dyuh know wie? Becuz yuh gut one on yuh back, dat's wie.

ENGLISHMAN: Do you know I'm dreadfully sorry, old man, but I haven't the least idea what you're talking about.

PLAINCLOTHESMAN: Can dat soikus stuff. Wutchuhgut in dat—(*He raps the trunk with his knuckles*)

ENGLISHMAN (*A light dawning*): Ah, I see. So that's what you call my trunk—

PLAINCLOTHESMAN: I calls dat uh trunk becuz dat is uh trunk, dat's wie.

ENGLISHMAN: But my dear chap, you're quite mistaken in supposing that to be a trunk.

PLAINCLOTHESMAN (*Menacingly*): Dat ain uh trunk?

ENGLISHMAN: I should say not. Dear, dear no. The very idea—ha-ha-ha.

PLAINCLOTHESMAN: Wal if dat ain uh trunk, will youse kinely tell me wut dat is?

ENGLISHMAN (*To himself*):—A trunk! That's really not half bad, you know. (*To the* PLAINCLOTHESMAN) But since you ask me, I don't mind telling you.

PLAINCLOTHESMAN: Wal, wut is it?

ENGLISHMAN: Why, that's my unconscious.

PLAINCLOTHESMAN (*Hand at ear*): Yuh wut?

ENGLISHMAN: My unconscious, old egg. Don't pretend you haven't heard of them in America.—Why, my dear boy, I was given to understand that a large percentage of them originated in the States: if I'm not mistaken, the one I've got is made hereabouts, in Detroit or some where like that.

PLAINCLOTHESMAN: Nevuh mine ware it wus made; wuts in it?

ENGLISHMAN: In it? *(He utters a profound sigh)* Ah—if I only knew. *(The* PLAINCLOTHESMAN *recoils in amazement. The* ENGLISH-MAN, *after uttering another and even more profound sigh, turns.)* Well, we can't know everything, can we. Cheerio! *(He starts out)*

PLAINCLOTHESMAN *(Leaping in front of the* ENGLISHMAN, *automatic in hand)*: HAY doan try dat stuff wid me. *(The* ENGLISHMAN *pauses)* Drop dat.

ENGLISHMAN *(Puzzled)*: Drop? What?

PLAINCLOTHESMAN: Drop wutchgut nmake it quick get me?

ENGLISHMAN *(Despairingly)*: I'm afraid I don't in the least know what you mean—

PLAINCLOTHESMAN: I mean leggo wid boat hans one after duhudder nleave duh res tuh gravity.

ENGLISHMAN: But you don't seem to understand—it's my—don't you realize? It's a part of myself—my unconscious—which you're asking me to let go of, to drop. Could anything be more impossibly ridiculous?

PLAINCLOTHESMAN: Sie lissun I doan givuh good god dam fuh youse "Un-con-shus." Nlemme tellyuh sumpn doan gimme no more uh youse lip rI'll make uh hole in youse.

ENGLISHMAN *(Agonized, wails)*: But I CAN'T—*(The* PLAINCLOTHES-MAN *fires: there is no explosion, but the* ENGLISHMAN *drops the trunk. As it lands, a terrific crash of broken glass is heard. The* ENGLISHMAN, *blinking, begins dusting himself, speaks severely.)* There—you see what you've done.

PLAINCLOTHESMAN *(Furiously)*: Wie dinchuh tell me day wuz booze in it yuh goddam fool! *(He rushes—dropping, in his haste, the automatic—at the trunk: falling on both knees, begins tearing at the lock: presently throws back the lid—starts—rising, recoiling, covers his eyes as if from an inconceivable horror: staggers back— falls. The* ENGLISHMAN *continues to dust himself. A* COP *hurries in with a drawn revolver.)*

COP: Hansup! *(The* ENGLISHMAN *puts up his hands)* Wuts dis? Uh trunk? *(He spies the* PLAINCLOTHESMAN, *who is lying on his face)* Sumun croaked—*(Pokes the prostrate figure with his foot)* Wie, it's Joe! *(Stooping, lifts the* PLAINCLOTHESMAN'S *left arm—releases it; the arm falls, inert)* Here's duh gun. *(Picks up the* PLAINCLOTHESMAN'S *automatic; drops it in the right outside pocket of the helpless* ENGLISHMAN'S *dinner jacket, and grimly faces his prey who immediately begins explaining)*

ENGLISHMAN: Yes you see I was carrying this when my bally topper fell off, and being quite unable to pick it up myself—the hat, that is—I asked this Joe as you call him if he'd mind awfully doing me the favour to help me.

COP: W-a-l.

ENGLISHMAN: Well he very kindly obliged me. But subsequently, owing to a perfectly ridiculous misunderstanding—more or less (I believe) as to the precise character of what I was carrying—

COP: Youse wus carryin—wut.

ENGLISHMAN *(Pointing at the trunk)*: This.

COP: HANSUP! *(The* ENGLISHMAN'S *hand flies aloft)* Wut for.

ENGLISHMAN: What for—O; well you see I'd heard that in the States it's practically impossible to get into a hotel with a woman without a bag.

COP *(Puzzled)*: How's dat? Say dem woids again.

ENGLISHMAN *(Raising his voice)*: I say: you see it's quite commonly known that in America one simply can't get into a hotel without a woman with a bag—I mean, get into a bag—I mean, get into a bag—no, no, get into a woman—

COP: Stop! Now yuh talkin doity.

ENGLISHMAN: I mean—it's jolly difficult to express the idea—

COP: Nevuh mine duh idear. Gowon.

ENGLISHMAN: —Well; and so, being as it happens extremely anxious to get into a hotel, I was for taking no chances—

COP: Ware's duh wummun.

ENGLISHMAN *(In astonishment)*: Woman? Did you say "woman"?

COP: Y-a-s.

ENGLISHMAN: What on earth do you mean, old egg? What woman?

COP: Duh wummun youse wus takin tuh duh hotel—is she in duh trunk?

ENGLISHMAN: In the trunk?—A woman? You're spoofing, old thing—

COP *(Approaching, bores the* ENGLISHMAN'S *entrails with the muzzle of the revolver)*: Kummon, wut wus youse carryin in duh trunk.

ENGLISHMAN: But—you don't seriously suppose I'd be such a bally ass as to carry a trunk on my back with a woman inside it!—A trunk—with a woman—on my back—ha-ha-ha; that's not half bad, you know—

COP *(Disgustedly, shoving the* ENGLISHMAN *aside)*: Get ovuh dare. *(He steps rapidly to the trunk—peers in; starts, gasps—recoils, dropping his revolver—and falls, lifeless, beside the trunk. Darkness.)*

VOICE OF HIM: Well?

VOICE OF ME: I liked the Englishman. But where were the eels?

VOICE OF HIM: The eels were in the tree.

VOICE OF ME: But I didn't see any tree.

VOICE OF HIM: There aren't any trees on 5th Avenue below 59th Street.

VOICE OF ME: Then what you said wasn't true.

VOICE OF HIM: But it wasn't untrue.

VOICE OF ME: Why not?

VOICE OF HIM: I said there weren't any mice, and there weren't. That was true, wasn't it?

VOICE OF ME: O yes—I'd forgotten about the mice.

VOICE OF HIM: And about the wheelbarrow too, I dare say?—But I hadn't.

VOICE OF ME: Why should you? After all, you invented it; and the two umbrellas and the tightrope and everything else. In fact, what's queer is, that I should have remembered those eels.

VOICE OF HIM: Allow me to remark that I consider your remembrance of those eels a great and definite compliment. Next we have. . . .

## Scene VII

SCENE: *A* U, *whose arms are alleys of distance and which is recognized as the promenade deck of a transatlantic liner seen from the bow.*

*At the end of each alley (or arm of the* U*) a rotund cigarsmoking* PASSENGER, *violently attired in an outrageous cap checked stockings and unblownnose breeches, is advancing with six balloons.*

*The two* PASSENGERS *meet in the foreground at the apex of the* U, *halt and converse. Each then explodes a balloon belonging to the other by touching it with his cigar, rounds the apex of the* U *and continues down the opposite side of the deck from which he emerged, until he reaches the end of his arm of the* U. *He then aboutfaces, retraverses this arm and arrives once more at the apex where he again meets the other* PASSENGER, *halts, converses, explodes a balloon and continues down the side of the deck from which he originally emerged.*

*The scene comprises six meetings, six conversations and the exploding of all the balloons. The questioning* PASSENGER *is played by the* DOCTOR.

FIRST CONVERSATION: What's new?—Nothing.

    Business?—Soso.

    Happy?—Not yet.

    Solong.—Solong.

SECOND CONVERSATION: What's new?—Nothing.

    Married?—Uh-huh.

    Children?—I dunno.

    Solong.—Solong.

THIRD CONVERSATION: What's new?—Nothing.

    Happy?—Soso.

    Retired?—Not yet.

    Solong.—Solong.

FOURTH CONVERSATION: What's new?—Nothing.

    Divorced?—Uh-huh.

    Blond?—I dunno.

    Solong.—Solong.

FIFTH CONVERSATION: What's new?—Nothing.

    Millionaire?—Soso.

    Happy?—Not yet.

    Solong.—Solong.

SIXTH CONVERSATION: What's new?—Nothing.

    Married?—Uh-huh.

    How long?—I dunno.

    Solong.—Solong.                  *(Darkness)*

VOICE OF ME: What was that about?

VOICE OF HIM: Chaos—not to be confused with manifold mendacities fakes counterfeit or spurious imitations such as Cosmos or commongarden ordinary unassuming Kolynos. Cheer up: The Other Play is almost played.

VOICE OF ME: What's coming now?

VOICE OF HIM *(Utters a profound sigh)*: Ah—if I only knew.

VOICE OF ME: Do you mean to say you don't know?

VOICE OF HIM: Excuse me: I was quoting.—The next scene, involving all sorts of allusions to subjects of unequal importance appertaining to the past the present and the future, calls for your undivided attention. I may add that it was composed by John Dewey—the world renowned authority on education and internationally famous author of such inspiring pamphlets as: "Into a Butterfly, or The Worm Will Turn"—in collaboration with C. Petronius, the talented writer of fairytales, on a desert island in the South Pacific during the eventful summer of 3, Eastern Standard Time, and deals in a vivid way with the loves of Spurius Lartius. . . .

## Scene VIII

SCENE: *The Old Howard's conception of a luxurious Roman villa, columns 'n' everything, with a protracted glimpse of Tiber and Coliseum plus a few mountains in what should be and is not the distance. Two centurions are shooting craps. Enter to them, lazily and unnoticed by them, an Ethiopian slave: he stands and regards the game with accumulating interest.*

ETHIOPIAN *(Finally beside himself with emotion)*: Dirry me.
FIRST CENTURION *(Looking up)*: Hello Sam. *(Picking up the dice, he rolls)*
SECOND CENTURION *(Also looking up)*: Hello Sam. Where yuh goin? *(He rolls)*
ETHIOPIAN: Hello boize. Ah ain goin nowhere.
FIRST CENTURION: Want to come in Sam? *(Rolls)*
ETHIOPIAN: Well ah doan mind if ah does. *(He produces an elaborate pocketbook)* How much you boize playin for?
BOTH CENTURIONS: Two bits.
ETHIOPIAN *(Producing a coin)*: Yoh faded. Now len me dem dice, fel-

lah, ah feels de speerit on me—*(He takes the dice from the* FIRST CENTURION; *heavenwarding his eyes, kisses the dice: murmurs)* All sweet ainjills come sit on deez two babies—. *(Rolls)*

SECOND CENTURION: You lose. *(Enter two* FAIRIES, *in scarlet togas, with lightningrods. The* CENTURIONS *nudge each other—hastily pick up the dice and start out)*

ETHIOPIAN *(Also going, murmurs en route, glancing at the* FAIRIES*)*: If daze anything worse dan Christians, it certainly am peddyrasts.

FIRST FAIRY *(Soprano)*: Where IS he.

SECOND FAIRY *(Calmly, alto)*: I don't know my dear.

FIRST: You were with him yesterday.

SECOND: I was not, dear. I haven't seen him since day before yesterday.

FIRST: You're lying to me, Tib.

SECOND: I am not, Claud.

FIRST: O dear O dear—I could just cry. *(He whimpers)*

SECOND *(Consolingly)*: Never mind, Claud darling.

FIRST: If he hadn't promised me; but he did—he absolutely promised me he'd be here at four o'clock sharp.

SECOND: He told ME four fifteen.

FIRST: O, so YOU'RE invited.

SECOND: Of course I'm invited. Why do you suppose I'm here, you stupid creature?

FIRST: Well, really—I think he might have told me. The very idea!— But I won't be treated this way, I won't stand it another instant, I won't, I WON'T—

SECOND: But listen dear—he didn't tell ME. . . .

FIRST: Tell you? What? What do you mean?

SECOND *(With dignity)*: That YOU would be here.

FIRST: I don't care. It's entirely different, with you. Besides, my nerves are on edge and everybody knows it—*(Enter a* THIRD, *portly* FAIRY*)*

THIRD FAIRY: Hello Tib dear. Hello Claud, what's the matter dear?

FIRST: It's just too awful.

THIRD *(Severely)*: Why is Claud crying, Tib? What HAVE you done?

SECOND: Now listen Con, I SWEAR I'm innocent. . . .

FIRST *(Sobbing)*: If—he—hadn't—promised—

THIRD: You mustn't cry this way, Claud, it ruins your complexion.

FIRST *(As before)*: I—know—it does.

THIRD: Here dear, take my handkerchief—just blow your nose and brace up. (CLAUD, *sobbing, blows his nose.*) That's better, isn't it.—Now tell me what's wrong between you and Tib.

SECOND: I SWEAR I'm innocent, Con, I SWEAR—

THIRD: Hello Tib dear. Hello Claud, what's the matter don't be afraid.

FIRST: It's . . . not Tib . . . it's—

SECOND: There now! Didn't I TELL you I was innocent?

THIRD *(Impatiently)*: Will you be still, Tibby?—What IS it Claud, tell Connie.

FIRST: O Con dear, I'm so nervous.

THIRD: Now don't be silly, Claud. Don't cry any more darling. I'm sure everything will be all right.

FIRST: He—he prom—

THIRD: Who promised?

FIRST: Suh—Caesar—

THIRD: Well, what about Caesar?

FIRST: —Pruh - promised he'd be—here at fuh - four sharp.

SECOND: He told me four fifteen. Are you invited?

THIRD: Invited? Of course. He's coming at four thirty.

FIRST: Coming! O, how w-o-n-d-e-r-f-u-l.

THIRD: There now, don't cry any more Claudie; everything will be all right.—By the way, have either of you girls read If Winter Comes?

SECOND: I haven't. It sounds lovely.

FIRST *(Cheering up)*: What a heavenly title.

THIRD: I just knew you'd want to read it, both of you—

SECOND: Have you got it on you, Con?

FIRST: Do give it to me first Con; you know I'm so nervous, I must have something to make me forget this horrible tragedy—

THIRD: It's Caesar's book, dear. He lent it to me yesterday to read.

SECOND: Lend it to me, Con—

FIRST: No, to me—

THIRD: I'd simply love to lend it to both of you if I had it, but I gave it back.

SECOND: That was horrid of you Con.

THIRD: Now Tib, I just couldn't help myself and you know I'm not to blame.

FIRST: But you might perfectly well have borrowed it for a long time; Caesar wouldn't have cared.

THIRD: Caesar will lend it to both of you girls, if you ask him nicely.— That's what I wanted to tell you before he arrives.

FIRST: O goody goody! I'm so nervous I just can't bear to wait another minute. *(Enter a* FOURTH, *excited* FAIRY)

FOURTH FAIRY: Hello Con, hello Tib and Claud: listen, have all you girls heard the news?

FIRST: What news, Gus dear?

FOURTH: Mercy, haven't you heard! Why it's all over town—

SECOND: What is?

THIRD: Tell us quickly, Gus.

FOURTH: —EVERYONE'S talking about it.

TRIO: Tell us, tell us—

FOURTH *(archly, finger at lip)*: Will you give me a big kiss, every one of you, if I tell—?

TRIO: Yes yes yes—. *(They cover him with kisses)* What is it?

FOURTH: Guess.

THIRD: Are the baths going to be renovated?

SECOND: Is Caesar sick?

FIRST *(Rapturously)*: Will he whip us?

FOURTH: No. You're ALL of you wrong, every one of you.

THIRD: WHAT is it?

FIRST: O you're so exasperating.

SECOND: It's just mean of you to keep it to yourself, Gus—

FOURTH *(Tantalizingly)*: Shall I tell?

TRIO: Yes yes yes.

FOURTH: All right. *(With enormous solemnity)* Daisy's dead.

TRIO: Dead!

SECOND: I don't believe it.

FIRST: I was with him only yesterday.

FOURTH: Well, he's dead.

THIRD: Impossible!

FIRST: How did he die?

FOURTH *(Proudly, with solemnity)*: Choked to death.

SECOND AND THIRD: O-o.

FIRST *(Rolling up his eyes and clasping his hands, murmurs rapturously)*:
What a b-e-a-u-t-i-f-u-l death! *(Trumpets without: enter majestically the onorevole* BENITO MUSSOLINI, *more or less in the costume
of Napoleon and with the traditional pose of that hero—"hands
locked behind, As if to balance the prone brow Oppressive with its
mind" (Browning)—but also wearing, at the end of a lightningrod,
a halo, probably in token of his Christlike role in raising Italia from
the dead. Changing his pose, he sticks one hand in his abdomen, à la
numerous portraits of the mighty Buonaparte.)*

FOUR FAIRIES *(Executing, more or less together, the fascist or Roman
salute)*: Hail, Caesar.

MUSSOLINI *(Who is played by the* DOCTOR*)*: Hello girls, have you
heard the news?

SECOND FAIRY *(Repeating the fascist salute)*: We have, Caesar.

FIRST *(Ditto)*: Gus told us, Caesar.

FOURTH *(Ditto)*: I told them, Caesar, about Daisy.

MUSSOLINI: Daisy be damned, shrimp.

FOUR FAIRIES *(Saluting)*: Aye, Caesar, aye.

MUSSOLINI: I'm talking about something important, damn it all.

THIRD FAIRY *(Timidly)*: If it is permitted to ask—have you lynched some more communists, Caesar?

FIRST *(Ecstatically)*: That would be just too wonderful!

MUSSOLINI: Lynched! I've roasted 'em alive, lozenge.

FOUR FAIRIES *(Whisper)*: O, w-o-n-d-e-r-f-u-l.

MUSSOLINI: Fifty today, sixty-nine yesterday, three hundred and forty-six the day before: that makes—six and nine are fifteen carry one, and four is five, eleven, five is sixteen, one and three is four—four hundred and sixty-five exactly, not including women and children.

FOUR FAIRIES *(As before)*: Div-ine.

MUSSOLINI: Nonsense, it's all a trick—anyone with brains can do it.

FOURTH FAIRY *(Involuntarily)*: O—no!

MUSSOLINI: I say they can, turnip! *(Wheeling, shouts)* CAMERIERI! *(Enter a saluting fascist)*

FASCIST: Aye Caesar.

MUSSOLINI: We know it's you.—A Mussolini special. *(Exit FASCIST, walking backwards with some difficulty and saluting at the same time)*

SECOND FAIRY *(Giggling embarrassedly)*: If it—if it is permit-

MUSSOLINI: Speak, thumbprint.

SECOND FAIRY *(Trembling)*: Can Caesar do—

MUSSOLINI: Caesar can do anything, nitwit. *(Re-enter FASCIST, bearing on a tray one liqueurglass and a fivegallon can which is labelled in huge black letters CASTOR OIL.* MUSSOLINI *takes the glass.)* Pour, slave. *(The* FASCIST *pours)*—Basta! *(Lifting the brimming glass,* MUSSOLINI *intones)* To S.M. II Re! *(*MUSSOLINI *and everyone else salute:* MUSSOLINI *drains the glass at a gulp—hands it to the* FASCIST, *who exits with tray, walking backwards and saluting* *with his left hand at the same time)* That's better! *(MUSSOLINI smacks his lips)* What was I saying, girls?

THIRD FAIRY: The news, Caesar.

MUSSOLINI: O yes; well I've forgotten now. Something of no importance—. *(A terrific crash, accompanied by screams, shrieks, screechings, shouts, gasps, grunts, groans, moans and similar expressions of woe, occurs and is immediately followed by piercing yells of "POLICE!" "MURDER!" "FIRE!"—The* FOUR FAIRIES *start almost out of their skins.)*

THIRD FAIRY: Whatever was that perfectly frightful noise!

SECOND: Wasn't it ghastly?

FIRST *(Whimpers)*: O I'm so nervous.

MUSSOLINI: CAMERIERI! *(Enter saluting* FASCIST*) What in Hell was that?*

FASCIST *(Saluting)*: Rome, Caesar.

FOURTH FAIRY: I was sure something terrible had happened—

MUSSOLINI: Silence, geranium!—What about Rome, slave? What's it making that noise for?

FASCIST *(Saluting)*: Rome can't help it, Caesar.

MUSSOLINI: Can't help it, onion!—Whaduhyuhmean Rome can't help it!

FASCIST *(Saluting)*: It's burning, Caesar.

FOUR FAIRIES: —Burning!—

MUSSOLINI *(Drawing himself up to his full majestic shortness roars)*: SILENZIO! *(The* FAIRIES *cringe before him: he surveys them with utter contempt—wheeling, speaks in a businesslike tone)* Knew I'd forgotten something.—Rome, of course. *(To* FASCIST.*)* Well, what are you waiting for?

FASCIST *(Saluting)*: The great Caesar's orders.

MUSSOLINI: Orders, my orders—yes, naturally. *(Removing his Napoleonic hat, scratches his head)* Pray to the Gods! And hurry up about it. *(The* FASCIST *backs salutingly off, colliding with an entering* MESSENGER *who, disentangling himself, falls on one knee, saluting)*

MESSENGER: Hail, Caesar, reign forever.

MUSSOLINI: Cough up, snowdrop, what's on your mind?

MESSENGER: My lord, the lady Popaea craves an audience.

MUSSOLINI: I don't get yuh, kid: slip it to me easy, I'm shortwaisted.

MESSENGER: Well——. *(Simpering)* She craves to see your highness.

MUSSOLINI: She ought to be ashamed of herself. Say that my highness is invisible.

MESSENGER: I have already said that, Caesar. *(He laughs foolishly)* Yet she persists, forsooth.

MUSSOLINI: Try again, old dear. Tell her I've got the mumps or something. *(A second frightful crash—followed by darkness)*

VOICE OF HIM: On the whole, how did that scene strike you?

VOICE OF ME: Not very favourably.

VOICE OF HIM: Really?

VOICE OF ME: You can see for yourself how silly it is to try to make a critic out of me.

VOICE OF HIM: I shall confine myself, however, to stating that your disapproval comes as a surprise; considering the all-pervading atmosphere of inherent spiritual nobility—not to mention the profound, deepspread, underlying religious significance of the thing. Possibly you didn't realize that those lads in the passionate nighties were Ecce Homos: the only lineal descendants of the ancient and honourable house of Savoy?

VOICE OF ME: I hate history.

VOICE OF HIM: So do I.—Europe, Africa, Asia: continents of Give. America: the land of Keep—Keep in step Keep moving Keep young Keep your head Keep in touch with events Keep smiling Keep your shirt on Keep off the grass Keep your arms and limbs inside the car. National disease: constipation. National recreation: the movies. National heroes: Abraham Lincoln who suppressed his own smut, George Washington who bought slaves with rum and Congressman Mann who freed the slaves. National anthem: You Forgot To Remember. National advertisement: The Spirit of '76—a man with a flag a man with a fife and a drummerboy—caption: General Debility Youthful Errors and Loss of Manhood . . . . Lettergo, professor!

## Scene IX

SCENE: *The stage as in Scene I.*

*Enter two figures, the* GENTLEMAN *(played by the* DOCTOR*) and the* INTERLOCUTOR *(played by* HIM.*)*

INTERLOCUTOR: On the whole, how does this city strike you?

GENTLEMAN: Strike me—are you inferring that I have defective eyesight? Do you think I'm mad? Eh?

INTERLOCUTOR: I wasn't inferring that—

GENTLEMAN: Strike me! *(He snorts)* How does it strike you—how does it strike anybody? *(With vast contempt)*—As a dungheap!

INTERLOCUTOR: There is a great deal of misery—

GENTLEMAN: Is there. I dare say.

INTERLOCUTOR: —Among the native population, I mean.

GENTLEMAN: Let me tell you something: between you and me, after looking this place over, what seems extraordinary is that the men and women who have to spend their lives in it don't all of them commit suicide.

INTERLOCUTOR: Many of them do.

GENTLEMAN: I know I should, if I had to stay here.

INTERLOCUTOR: I take it this is your first visit—?

GENTLEMAN: Yes, and my last.

INTERLOCUTOR: Yes. And I can assure you that before the war this city was not only very gay but even beautiful.

GENTLEMAN: Damitall, that's what I always heard—and here I go out of my way to come; and what do I find? A few motheaten streets and a couple of rusty restaurants. *(Philosophically)* Serves me right. That's what a fellow gets in this world when he takes anybody else's word for anything.

INTERLOCUTOR: But my dear sir, you forget the war—times have changed—you see before you the fruits of defeat—

GENTLEMAN *(Vehemently)*: I do forget the war. And what's more, I see no reason why everybody else shouldn't. It would be a damn good thing for some of these people if they turned over a new leaf and showed a little life! Why, look here—. *(He plunges a hand into his outside jacket pocket: produces a fistful of paper money)* Look at this—

INTERLOCUTOR: Poo.

GENTLEMAN: Pooh nothing; it's no joke, let me tell you—why a fellow needs a trunk to carry a nickel's worth—

INTERLOCUTOR: You misunderstand me: I'm telling you that the unit of currency here is the poo.

GENTLEMAN: O, I see: poo—yes, of course.

INTERLOCUTOR: Do you know what the poo was equivalent to, before the war?

GENTLEMAN *(Nettled)*: I don't know and I don't care! It's worthless now—

INTERLOCUTOR: Worthless? No; not exactly. Do you know what a mill is?

GENTLEMAN: I'll say I do. My old man made his dough in 'em. O boy.

INTERLOCUTOR: I meant another kind—we were speaking of currency: a mill in American money is the tenth part of a cent.

GENTLEMAN: O, currency—tenth part, sure. I get you.

INTERLOCUTOR: Well: if a mill were a hundred dollars, if it WERE— you understand?

GENTLEMAN: Hundred dollars, sure.

INTERLOCUTOR: A poo, at the present rate of exchange, would be worth slightly less than half of one-eighth of the sixteenth part of one mill.

GENTLEMAN: Hm. Yes. I dare say. Terrible, isn't it.

INTERLOCUTOR: It's a great deal more terrible than you or I imagine. But speaking of the war—

GENTLEMAN *(Turning on him, cries petulantly)*: The war? The war's over, isn't it?

INTERLOCUTOR: Not in this part of the world, my friend. You have only to look about you to realize that—

GENTLEMAN: O well, if it isn't it ought to be, and remembering it won't do anybody any good—you'll agree to that?

INTERLOCUTOR: But one has to realize that people everywhere are hungry—that there are riots almost daily—

GENTLEMAN: Riots? What do you mean?

INTERLOCUTOR: I mean that people are rioting.

GENTLEMAN: You mean people are rioting—here are people, you and I, neither of whom (unless I'm very much mistaken) can be said by the most ignorant and uninformed person to be rioting.

INTERLOCUTOR: I refer to the poor. The unemployed. There are five hundred thousand of them in this city with nothing to eat, I believe.

GENTLEMAN: Do you? Let me tell you something: I believe nothing the newspapers say.

INTERLOCUTOR: It's a fact. I saw at least ten thousand only a few days ago—Monday, it was—demonstrating in front of the Crystal Hotel.

GENTLEMAN: Did you indeed. That happens to be my hotel.

INTERLOCUTOR: You have just moved in, perhaps?

GENTLEMAN: No, worse luck.

INTERLOCUTOR: May I ask how long you've been stopping at that hotel?

GENTLEMAN: You may. I've been there ever since I arrived. I arrived, lemme see: yes—last Saturday. I shall leave next Saturday. I should leave this minute if there was a decent train.

INTERLOCUTOR: The demonstration which I saw in front of your hotel occurred last Monday at about eleven in the morning.

GENTLEMAN: I saw nothing unusual at eleven in the morning. In fact, if I remember correctly, I was in bed at eleven in the morning.

INTERLOCUTOR: And you heard nothing unusual?

GENTLEMAN: I heard a mild rumpus of some sort—nothing to disturb myself about.

INTERLOCUTOR: A few weeks ago, I believe, they smashed your hotel and held up all the occupants, ladies included.

GENTLEMAN: I believe nothing unless I see it.—And do you believe the occupants of my hotel gave them anything?

INTERLOCUTOR: Several billion poo and a few thousand dollars . . . of course, the crowd may not have held up the people in bed; I don't know about that. The wisest thing, under the circumstances, might be to go to bed and stay there.

GENTLEMAN: My dear chap, I stay in bed when it pleases me to stay in bed; and I get up when I like to get up; and I read all the newspapers I can find—few enough, Heaven knows, in this godforsaken place—

INTERLOCUTOR: —And which you can understand.

GENTLEMAN: I beg your pardon?

INTERLOCUTOR: —All the newspapers in English.

GENTLEMAN: Naturally. What else should I read?—But as I was saying: I read them all, and I believe not a word in any of them.

INTERLOCUTOR: Then may I ask why you read them?

GENTLEMAN: Because in a hole like this there's nothing else to do. Besides which, let me tell you something: it rather amuses me to see how consistently they contradict each other. (*A dull booming hum is heard: the noise grows, thickens—within it, noises appear and disappear)*

INTERLOCUTOR: If, as I am led to believe, you enjoy seeing things for yourself, all you need do is wait here a few minutes. Because— do you hear that?

GENTLEMAN: I hear a noise; or if you like, I hear noises.

INTERLOCUTOR: Exactly. They're coming.

GENTLEMAN: They? Who's they?

INTERLOCUTOR: The mob.

GENTLEMAN: Well?

INTERLOCUTOR: Excuse me. I'm running along. In my experience, it's best to give these people a large berth.

GENTLEMAN: In that case, let me tell you something: I shall sit here and wait.

INTERLOCUTOR: Listen, don't be a fool: this is no laughing matter— clear out. *(The noises multiply, the noise deepens)* It's damned dangerous.

GENTLEMAN: Clear out? I shall do nothing of the kind. On the contrary, I shall sit on this box and watch this mob, as you call it. *(He sits down placidly on an old box)*

INTERLOCUTOR: Man! You're crazy—you don't know what you're doing. *(He tugs at the* GENTLEMAN'S *arm)*

GENTLEMAN: Although by your account crazy, I am sufficiently possessed of my senses to inquire why you don't go, if you don't want to stay?

INTERLOCUTOR: Idiot!—*(He stands irresolute, perplexed)* Here. *(He grabs out of his trouser pocket a minute gnarled loaf of coarse blackish bread. Shoves it into the* GENTLEMAN'S *hands.)*

GENTLEMAN: Why are you presenting me with this? *(He regards it distrustfully)* What is it?

INTERLOCUTOR: Bread you ass—it may save your life. Take it.

GENTLEMAN: Thanks, I'm not hungry. *(He inspects the loaf)* And if I were, I should not feel particularly inclined to eat this.

INTERLOCUTOR: You fool—throw it to them and run! *(He runs for his life, as a mob—roaring, muttering, gesticulating—swarms upon the stage and curiously, gradually, fatally forms a semicircle to include the GENTLEMAN: beside whom, an immensely tall greenish mouldering SHAPE quaveringly spews itself upward)*

SHAPE: I'm hungry.

GENTLEMAN: Have you got anything to eat?

SHAPE: No.

GENTLEMAN: Then how foolish of you to be hungry—whereas, if you had something to eat, there'd be some sense in being hungry. *(The greenish tall mouldering shape collapsingly sinks back into the mob: a SECOND SHAPE, bluish and abrupt, emerges)*

SECOND SHAPE: I have nothing to eat.

GENTLEMAN: Why don't you eat nothing then? Do you want to be hungry? *(The SECOND SHAPE darts back into the mob. A WOMAN appears in its place.)*

WOMAN: Give me a little piece of your bread.

GENTLEMAN *(Regarding her suspiciously)*: How little a piece?

WOMAN: A crumb.

GENTLEMAN: A crumb indeed. What will a crumb do?

WOMAN: It will make me live for an hour.

GENTLEMAN: Ridiculous—if what you say were true, one could, simply by eating crumbs, live forever. *(Severely)* Don't forget, my dear woman, that there is such a thing as death. *(The WOMAN disappears: an OLD WOMAN stands before the GENTLEMAN)*

OLD WOMAN: I'm dying.

GENTLEMAN: Are you? That's apropos of you.

OLD WOMAN: Dying yes. *(She nuzzles against him)* Do you understand?

GENTLEMAN *(Drawing back)*: No I don't. And do you want to know why? Because, let me tell you something: I'm not dying myself.

*(The* OLD WOMAN *falls and is swept back into the mob, whose elements gyrate, intercreep and writhingly focus: a twisted whitish* SHAPE *spouts out)*

THIS SHAPE *(Pointing)*: Bread.

GENTLEMAN: Yes, that's bread. Well?

THIS SHAPE: Give.

GENTLEMAN: Give what?

THIS SHAPE: Bread.

GENTLEMAN: Why should I—what's bread for?

THIS SHAPE: Eat.

GENTLEMAN: Quite right. Bread is to eat; in giving my bread, instead of eating it, I should, therefore, be doing something quite unspeakably stupid. *(*THIS SHAPE *spouts into the mob: a* WHORE, *hollow, dilapidated, swims forward, ogling)*

WHORE *(Simpers)*: Give me just a tiny nibble, dearie. I'll give you something very nice for it, darling.

GENTLEMAN: Well now, that's sensible. That's talking business. You're not like the rest of them. You're businesslike, intelligent: you make me a business proposition. Well, let's hear it: just what is your proposition?

WHORE: Give me the tiniest nibble and I'll give you one deep big nice kiss.

GENTLEMAN: Your proposition interests me. Let's go on with it: what will you give me for a big nibble?

WHORE: For a big nibble I'll let you kiss me till you're tired.

GENTLEMAN *(Holds up the loaf before her, speaks slowly)*: And what would you do if I should give you all of this bread?

WHORE *(Shrugging)*: I'd give some of it away. I couldn't eat that much bread. *(A* FOURTH SHAPE, *elbowing her violently aside, stands)*

GENTLEMAN *(Angrily, to* FOURTH SHAPE*)*: Who are you?

FOURTH SHAPE: A human being.

GENTLEMAN *(With severity)*: A being, my friend, is someone who exists; a being is someone alive. What makes you think that you're alive?

FOURTH SHAPE: I'm hungry.

GENTLEMAN: In that case, let me tell you something: what you say is sheer nonsense. Look at me—I'm not hungry. And I'm alive.

FOURTH SHAPE: No. You're not.

GENTLEMAN: What do you mean?

FOURTH SHAPE (*Slowly*): You're not alive.

GENTLEMAN: Of course I'm alive. Aren't people who eat bread alive?

FOURTH SHAPE: You're. Not eating. Bread.

GENTLEMAN: Because I'm not hungry, I'm not eating it now: I prefer to save it. But I assure you I shall eat it eventually, because I'm alive and this is bread.

FOURTH SHAPE (*Shakes his dark, gnarled face to left and right*): That's. Not. Bread.

GENTLEMAN: I never in all my life heard such drivel. And if it's not bread, pray what is it?

FOURTH SHAPE (*A slender mutilated finger, poking from one ragged too long sleeve and gliding toward his filthy breast, points at his heart*): Me.

GENTLEMAN: All right then. In that case, it's more sensible that I should eat you than that you should eat yourself. (*He turns away*)

FOURTH SHAPE: Dead people don't. Need to eat.

GENTLEMAN (*Pettishly*): But I'm NOT dead, my dear fellow. On the contrary. I'm very much alive.

FOURTH SHAPE: Dead. You're dead, yes.

GENTLEMAN (*Shrugging*): The man is crazy. Here I am sitting not two feet away from him holding a piece of bread, and he tells me I'm dead. Why, you fool, I'm no more dead than yourself, in fact much less so.

FOURTH SHAPE: I'm hungry. (*His handless scarecrow sleeves gesture*) We're all hungry.

VOICES: Hungry. Yes. Eat.

GENTLEMAN (*Indignantly*): And what of that? Suppose you all ARE hungry and I'm not: what the devil difference does THAT make?

FOURTH SHAPE: You're not. Hungry. Only dead people. Aren't hungry.

GENTLEMAN: This is idiotic. You don't know what you're talking about, that's the whole truth of the matter—you can't listen to reason.

FOURTH SHAPE: Listen to me. I'll make you alive.

GENTLEMAN: No thanks. My mother did that for me, some time ago.

FOURTH SHAPE: I'll be your mother. Give me your bread. I'll make you alive.

GENTLEMAN: Give you my bread, eh? What would you do with my bread if I should give it to you?—Would you eat it?

FOURTH SHAPE: Eat. Bread. Yes.

GENTLEMAN: Then by your own account you'd be dead, stupid— nobody wants to be dead.

FOURTH SHAPE: I Want to be dead.

GENTLEMAN: O do you? Well, that's no reason why I should murder you.

FOURTH SHAPE: Yes, it's a reason

GENTLEMAN: Now look here: I don't much fancy the idea of murdering somebody—

FOURTH SHAPE (*Pointing at his heart*): Look.—Here.

GENTLEMAN: Yes, it's very dirty.—And furthermore, I see no reason why I should be a murderer against my will.

FOURTH SHAPE (*Hoisting abruptly his sleeves, assumes the position of one crucified. As he does so, hands emerge.*): Murder. Me. Please. (*A rush of shapes around him: wallowing squirming wrestling to offer themselves—all stretching out their arms, all crying "Kill me!"*)

MOTHER WITH A CHILD: Kill my baby before you kill the others; please kill my baby first.

VOICE: No, me first.

ANOTHER VOICE: Me.

GENTLEMAN (*Rising, stands: trembling.—Furiously screams out.*): Am I God that I should strike you all dead?

MULTITUDE OF SHAPES (*In three huge cries*): Yes. You are God. Yes.

GIRL'S VOICE (*Shrill*): You are God himself.

A DARK VOICE: God is a man with a piece of bread.

GENTLEMAN: What is the—I don't—really, I don't understand you people—are you all crazy? Or am I crazy?

MULTITUDE OF SHAPES (*Together*): You are dead.

GENTLEMAN (*Utters a trivial brief cry*): Then damitall, kill yourselves! (*He hurls the loaf. The mass of pouncing scrambling wrestling screaming yearning shapes squirmingly bulges toward the missile; revolving furiously within itself, and rumbling choking roaring, gradually disappears. Snow begins falling. The* GENTLEMAN *stands for a minute, confused—presses his hands to his head in a brittle gesture. He sits down and stares before him, with arms folded. After a minute, his hands automatically begin unbuttoning the buttons of his waistcoat. Rising, staring fixedly at the audience, he takes off his jacket—drops it to one side. Then he takes off his waistcoat and drops it on top of his jacket. Sitting down, he begins automatically unlacing one shoe. A* POLICEMAN *timidly enters.*)

POLICEMAN (*Saluting, speaks with the utmost respect*): Pardon me, sir. May I ask what you are doing?

GENTLEMAN (*Looking up with vague eyes, does not stop unlacing*): Yes, I'm taking off my clothes.

POLICEMAN: Excuse me, sir; if I'm not mistaken it's rather cold to be undressing, isn't it?—It's snowing, sir, I believe.

GENTLEMAN (*Without looking up*): I can't help it. (*The snow falls more rapidly*)

POLICEMAN: Of course not, sir! But mightn't it be better to wait till you got home? *(Coaxingly)* It would be warmer, sir, much warmer.

GENTLEMAN: I can't wait—I mustn't wait. *(He jerks off one shoe: dropping it, begins unlacing rapidly the other)* I'm late already.

POLICEMAN: Beg pardon sir, for asking a question—if I may be so bold, why couldn't it wait? *(The* GENTLEMAN, *jerking off the other shoe, holds it in both hands. His eyes lift to the* policeman's *face. Dropping the shoe, he rises suddenly; stands, staring into the embarrassed eyes before him—the* POLICEMAN *blushes.)* Beg pardon; I mean (excuse me, sir, for suggesting)—it might be a trifle more decent.

GENTLEMAN *(In a low voice)*: In that case, let me tell you something. *(Leaning toward the* POLICEMAN, *whispers loudly)* I've. Just. Been. Born. *(Hurriedly slips the suspenders from his shoulders—in another instant he steps quickly and automatically from his trousers. The* POLICEMAN *staggers. The* GENTLEMAN *drops his trousers: pauses, irresolute: after shivering doubtfully for a few seconds, he demands plaintively.)* If you please, what do babies wear? *(The* POLICEMAN *quakes)* Very little babies? *(The* POLICEMAN *totters; pulling from his left hippocket a crucifix, clamps it in fervent fists. He falls on his knees, shutting his eyes, and removes his hat into which a great deal of snow immediately falls.)*

POLICEMAN *(Simply)*: Now I lay me down to sleep. . . .

• CURTAIN •

# ACT THREE

## Scene I

SCENE: *The room of Act One, further revolved so that the fourth or invisible wall is the door wall. The wall to the audience's right (corresponding to the door wall of Act One Scene 4) is the solid wall. The middle wall is the mirror wall. The window wall is to the audience's left.* HIM'S *hat lies on the centre of the table where the automatic was lying at the end of Act One Scene 4.*

ME *and* HIM *are seated at opposite ends of the sofa which is against the solid wall to the audience's right.*

ME: Where I am I think it must be getting dark: I feel that everything is moving and mixing, with everything else.

HIM: I feel that it's very dark.

ME: Do you—feel?

HIM: Terribly dark.

ME: Are you a little afraid of the dark?

HIM: I've always been. *(The room darkens rapidly)* May I sit beside you?

ME: If you don't very much mind. *(He does so)*

HIM: A hand. Accurate and incredible.

ME *(To herself)*: The dark is so many corners—

HIM: Here life is, moves; faintly. A wrist. The faint throb of blood, precise, miraculous.

ME *(As before)*: —so many dolls, who move—

HIM: Curve. And they talk of dying! The blood delicately descending and ascending: making an arm. Being an arm. The warm flesh, the dim slender flesh filled with life, slenderer than a miracle, frailer.

ME *(As before)*: —by Themselves.

HIM: These are the shoulders through which fell the world. The dangerous shoulders of Eve, in god's entire garden newly strolling. How young they are! They are shy, shyest, birdlike. Not shoulders, but young alert birds. *(The figures of ME and HIM are almost invisible)*

ME *(Almost inaudibly)*: Darker

HIM: A distinct throat. Which breathes. A head: small, smaller than a flower. With eyes and with lips. Lips more slender than light; a smile how carefully and slowly made, a smile made entirely of dream. Eyes deeper than Spring. Eyes darker than Spring, more new.

ME *(To herself)*: We must go very carefully . . .

HIM: These, these are the further miracles—

ME *(Almost inaudibly)*: . . . gradually . . .

HIM: —the breasts. Thighs. The All which is beyond comprehension—the All which is perpetually discovered, yet undiscovered: sexual, sweet. Alive!

ME *(Faintly)*: . . . until light. *(Complete darkness. After a few moments her voice whispers with a sort of terror.)*

VOICE OF ME: What are you saying.

VOICE OF HIM *(Subdued, intense, trembling)*: Not saying: praying . . . *(The voice hardens)* . . . now I lay you down to not sleep—. *(Silence. Then a scream: the room suddenly opens into total visibility. ME stands—tense erect panting—beside the sofa on which HIM sprawls.)*

ME: No!

HIM *(Slowly collecting himself rises slowly)*: Are you sure? Are you terribly, wonderfully sure?

ME: Sure. Yes. (*A pause. She walks upstage to the mirror. He crosses the room to the table; takes and lights a cigarette.*)

HIM (*Standing at the window, laughs briefly*): Mademoiselle d'Autrefois, purveyor of mental meanderings and bodily bliss to Ahsh E. M. His Imperial Majesty, the Man in the Mirror!

ME (*At the mirror*): What do you mean.

HIM: I mean—. (*Twirls the match out*)—That you have been the mistress of someone.

ME: Are you terribly, wonderfully sure?

HIM: Of that? Yes. I am sure.

ME: I gave him everything, you mean?

HIM: I mean just that. Once upon a time.

ME: How extraordinary—and who were you, once upon a time?

HIM (*Flicks the ash*): Why do you ask?

ME: Because—shall I tell you?

HIM: If you wish.

ME: The more I remember, the more I am sure it never happened.

HIM (*Simply*): Dead.

ME (*Turning from the mirror, walks toward him slowly*): And now everything changes. And I can distinguish between things. O, I begin to see things very clearly.—You are just as you were.

HIM: I understand less and less.

ME: Do you? It's clear now—can't you see?

HIM: My eyes are very bad today as the blind man said.

ME: That's what he said. (*Stands before him*) And this is what you say: "May I kiss you?"

HIM: I say that to whom? . . . Excuse me; will you have a cigarette?

ME (*Refuses with a curt gesture*): You simply say it.

HIM: I am very dull. . . . May I kiss you?

ME: No. Because I'm not, any more—this isn't me. But somewhere me is, and it would be jealous if you kissed somebody else.

HIM (*Cutting a laugh in two*): "Jealous"! Why not the truth?

ME: You are making a mistake.

HIM: Probably.

ME: There's nobody else. Really: so far as I know.

HIM: I should prefer that you did not lie to me.

ME: Yes?

HIM: I should.

ME *(She looks entirely at him)*: I'm not lying.

HIM *(Looking intently at her)*: No, you're not lying.

ME *(Quietly)*: The snow did it, or it was the rain—Something outside of me and you: and we may as well let Something alone. *(She walks toward the sofa)*

HIM: That would be pleasant to believe.

ME *(To herself)*: Which moves quietly, when everything is asleep; folding hands . . . I don't know. Shutting flowers I guess, putting toys away. *(She sits, in one corner of the sofa)*

HIM: This is the end?

ME: Do you like to call it that?

HIM: Tell me, what is it, if it isn't the end?

ME: This might be where we begin.

HIM: To begin hurts. *(A pause)* Do you think that this folding and shutting Person, who moves, can take memories away?

ME: No. *(A pause. She smiles.)*—I feel as if we'd never lived: everything is so sure, so queer. *(Another pause)*

HIM: Everything will be queerer perhaps.

ME: Do you think?

HIM: When everything has stopped.

ME: Stopped?

HIM: When I and you are—so to speak—folded, with all our curves and gestures.

ME: —In the earth?

HIM *(Strolls toward the sofa)*: Anywhere.

ME: Somewhere, in the Spring, you and I lying . . . together. . . .

HIM: And so exceedingly still.

ME *(Smiles, shaking her head)*: No: there'll be things.

HIM *(Sitting opposite her)*: Things?

ME: Trees pushing. And little creatures wandering busily in the ground, because everywhere it's Spring. *(Smiles)* They will go wandering into me and into you, I expect—roots and creatures and things—but I shan't mind.

HIM: No.

ME *(In a low voice)*: If I'm with you.

HIM *(In a low voice)*: It will all be gone then; then it will be too late. Think.

ME: . . . I don't want to think.

HIM: Lips, which touched—at first how lightly! What were lips distinctly slowly coming against more than lips; mouths, firmly living upon each other: the focused Ourselves (alive proud deep bewildered) approaching gradually. Nearing, exquisitely and scarcely. Touching. And then—heartily announced by miles, by years, of strutting light—the minute instant, the enormous Now. . . . *(Pauses; smiles)* Only think, dear, of you and of me gone, like two kites when the string breaks, positively into nowhere. Shut like umbrellas. Folded like napkins.

ME *(Looking at him and away, speaks softly)*: Only think, dear, that you and I have never been really in love. Think that I am not a bit the sort of person you think. Think that you fell in love with someone you invented—someone who wasn't me at all. Now you are trying to feel things; but that doesn't work, because the nicest things happen by themselves. You can't make them happen. I can't either, but I don't want to. And when you try to make them happen, you don't really fool yourself and certainly you don't fool me. That's one thing about me. I'm not clever and I don't try to make things happen.—Well, you made a mistake about me and I know that. But the fact is, you know you made a mistake. Everybody knows it. . . . Think what is: think that you are now talking very beautifully through your hat.

HIM *(His glance travels to the table and returns to her)*: You are a very remarkable person—among other reasons, because you can make me afraid.

ME: I'm not, and I don't want to be, remarkable. What you really think about me—and won't admit that you think—is true.

HIM: Don't you understand—

ME: I don't. I feel. That's my way and there's nothing remarkable about it: all women are like that.

HIM: Noone is like you.

ME: Pooh. I don't flatter myself—not very much. I know perfectly well it's foolish of you to waste your time with me, when there are people who will understand you. And I know I can't, because things were left out of me.—What's the use of being tragic? You know you aren't sad, really. You know what you really are, and really you're always sure of yourself: whereas I'm never sure.—If anybody were going to be tragic it ought to be me. I know that perfectly well. I've never done anything and I don't believe I ever will. But you can do things. Noone can make you unsure of yourself. You know you will go on, and all your life you've known.

HIM *(Trembling, looks at his hands)*: May I tell you a great secret?

ME: A secret?

HIM: All my life I've wondered if I am any good. If my head and my heart are made out of something firmer or more living than what I see everywhere covering itself with hats and with linen.—If all the capable and little and disgusting minds which, somehow, are responsible for the cities and the countries in which I exist, have not perhaps also manufactured this thing— this bundle of wishes—which I like to call "myself." If my arms dreams hands exist with an intensity different from or beyond the intensity of any other arms dreams hands. . . . You cannot imagine how disagreeable it is to wonder—to look about you, at the eyes and the gestures which promenade themselves in streets and in houses, and to be afraid. To think: "Am I also one of these, a doll, living in a doll world, doomed to be undressed, dressed, spanked, kissed, put to bed?" *(Trembling, wipes carefully with his handkerchief a sweating forehead)* You can't imagine how disagreeable it is. Suppose that you spent your life buying a dress. Suppose that at last you found the precise and wonderful dress which you had dreamed of, and suppose that you bought it and put it on and walked in it everywhere and everywhere you saw thousands of people all of whom were wearing your dress.

ME: You mean I'm like everybody else.

HIM *(Fiercely)*: I mean that you have something which I supremely envy. That you are something which I supremely would like to discover: knowing that it exists in itself as I do not exist and as I never have existed. How do I know this? Because through you I have come to understand that whatever I may have been or may have done is mediocre. *(Bitterly)* You have made me realize that in the course of living I have created several less or more interesting people—none of whom was myself.

ME *(With a brief gesture)*: O dear. Am I like that?

HIM: Like nothing.

ME: Please don't talk to me this way. I really don't understand. And I think you don't understand me, very well . . . nothing is sure.

HIM *(Rising, smiles)*: Limbo, the without pain and joyless unworld, lady. In one act: or, my life is made of glass.

ME *(Rising, moves; stands beside him)*: Your—what?

HIM *(Carefully looking into her helpless lifted eyes, speaks carefully)*: I mean a clock ticking. Words which were never written. Cries heard through a shut window. Forgotten. Winter. Flies hanging mindless to walls and ceiling around a stove. Laughter of angels.

Eheu fugaces. Glass flowers. *(He walks to the table and picks up his hat. Turning, makes for the invisible door.* ME *steps in front of him quickly.)*

ME: I have no mind. I know that. I know I'm not intelligent, and that you liked me for something else. There isn't any sense in my asking—I ask merely because I want to. I know I haven't any brains and really I don't care. I've seen women with brains and they're miserable, or anyway they look so—I don't know; it might be nice to have a mind sometimes. Please don't think I'm unhappy, because I'm not, and I'm not trying to make you unhappy. I know what I'm really like and what's more I know that you know—we're not fooling ourselves. But what you're really like I don't know; and that doesn't make me unhappy either: I don't care. I know part of you and I'm glad. As a matter of fact I'm rather proud. I think I know a great deal—for instance, if I ask you something you won't mind. And if my asking hurt you, I wouldn't care—I'm like that; it's me. I'm glad everything's over: because I've loved you very much, I'm glad there'll be nothing except memories. . . . You know what I liked best about you, what I will always like and will always remember. It's your hands—you know that and I tell you. Tell me something. Because it doesn't matter and you're going, tell me one thing. Tell me (as if I was dead and you were talking to someone else with your hands on her breasts) what there was, once, about me.

HIM *(After a short pause)*: I hoped that I had—perhaps—told you.

ME: Listen. *(Earnestly, staring with entire seriousness into his eyes, almost whispers)* It's snowing: think. Just think of people everywhere and houses and rivers and trees and the mountains and oceans. Then think of fingers—millions—out of somewhere quietly and quickly coming, hurrying very carefully. . . . Think of everywhere fingers touching; fingers, skillfully gently everything—O think of the snow coming down beautifully and beautifully frightening ourselves and turning dying and love and the world and me and you into five toys. . . . Touch me a little. *(Taking his right wrist, she puts its hand against her dress)* It will be so pleasant to dream of your hands. For a hundred years.

HIM *(Whispers)*: Dreams don't live a hundred years.

ME: Don't they? *(Smiles. Lets his wrist, hand, drop.)* Perhaps mine does. *(Strolling to the table, opens the box; taking, lights a cigarette; quickly blows out the match)* It's very late, I think. *(His shutting face whitens—putting on his hat, he goes out through the invisible door; stands, facing the audience.* ME *unsteadily crosses the room to the sofa. Darkness.)*

VOICE OF ME: If I had a mind, every morning I'd jump out of bed and hurry to a sort of secret drawer, where I kept my mind because someone might steal it. Then I'd open the drawer with a key and find my mind safe. But to make sure, I'd take it out of the box where it lived—because if I had a mind I'd be very careful of it for fear it might break—and I'd go to the window with this little mind of mine, and holding it very carefully I'd look through the window out over the roofs (with smoke coming up out of all the chimneys slowly and maybe a street where people moved carefully in the sunlight, in the morning).

## Scene II

SCENE: *The three rocking knitting* FIGURES, *facing the picture with their backs to the audience. Both heads are in the picture and the* WOMAN'S *eyes are closed.*

FIRST FIGURE: I held my husband up to the light yesterday and saw through him.

SECOND: What did you see?

THIRD: Your Hole appearance depends upon your hair.

FIRST: I saw father eating a piece of asparagus.

SECOND: Your husband's a landscape gardener?

THIRD: It's off because it's out.

FIRST: Not exactly. He does something in the interests of science.

SECOND: Really?—What does he do?

FIRST: I'm not quite sure . . . something about guineapigs I think.

SECOND: About guineapigs? How fascinating.

THIRD: Happiness in every box.

FIRST: Yes I think he does something to them so they'll have children—

SECOND: Not really!

THIRD: A pure breath is good manners.

FIRST: —because you see he wants them to have children in the interests of science.

SECOND: How remarkable. I didn't suppose guineapigs COULD have children.

FIRST: I didn't either when I married him, but George says he doesn't see why guineapigs can't have children if children can have guineapigs.

THIRD: A clean tooth never decays.

SECOND: DO children have guineapigs?

FIRST: O yes, more's the pity. Mine often have it.

THIRD: Your nails show your refinement.

SECOND: Badly?


## Scene III

SCENE: *Au Père Tranquille (Les Halles). Whores asleep. Music asleep. A waiter asleep. Two customers, a* BLOND GONZESSE *and the* GEN-TLEMAN *of Act Two, Scene 9, sit side by each at a corner table on which are two whiskies and an ashreceiver. A bell rings violently and a* HEADWAITER *rushes into the room.*

HEADWAITER: Psst! *(Exit. The whores yawn, roll off the chairs and begin dancing with one another half asleep. The pianist, starting to a sitting position, bangs out chords—the violinist, reaming his eyes, breaks into tune—the drummer, shoving back his hair, swats the cymbals. Awakened by this racket, the waiter gets up and adjusts his tie in a mirror: turning, moves glasses aimlessly here and there on tables.* TWO FEMALE VOICES *are heard in the vicinity of the doorway.)*

FIRST FEMALE VOICE: Of course I know him. He's the man from whom Belasco steals his ideas.

SECOND FEMALE VOICE: Steals whose ideas?

FIRST FEMALE VOICE: Belasco's. *(The owners of the voices, a* FAIRLY YOUNG WOMAN *and an* OLDER WOMAN, *enter, followed by the obsequiously ushering* HEADWAITER*)*

HEADWAITER *(Making, unnoticed by the new arrivals, a sign of negation to music and whores)*: Bon soir mesdames. Par ici mesdames? *(He guides his prey to a table in the centre of the room. The whores and music cease their activities and resume their slumbers.)*

OLDER: Boan swaah.

HEADWAITER *(Ostantatiously presenting menus, as the new arrivals seat themselves)*: Voici mesdames. *(Placing himself at the* OLDER'S *elbow, he obsequiously threatens)* Qu'est-ce que c'est mesdames? *(Both women pick up menus. Both study their menus attentively)*

OLDER *(Absentmindedly)*: Let me see. . . . *(She adjusts a lorgnette)* Y-e-s. *(Looking up)* Donny mwah un omb.

HEADWAITER *(Feigning pleasure)*: Un homme. Très bien. Et pour madame?

FAIRLY YOUNG *(Flustered)*: What are you having Sally?

OLDER *(Laying down menu and lowering lorgnette)*: An omb, dear, as usual.

FAIRLY YOUNG: That's not a bad idea. *(Engagingly)* I'll have the same.

OLDER *(Interpreting)*: Ong kore un omb.

HEADWAITER *(As before)*: Ca fait deux hommes; bien mesdames. *(To OLDER)* Et comment madame désire-t-elle son homme?

OLDER *(Without hesitation)*: Stewed, seal voo play.

HEADWAITER *(To FAIRLY YOUNG)*: Et madame?

FAIRLY YOUNG: What does he want to know?

OLDER: He says how do you want your omb.

FAIRLY YOUNG *(Puzzled and embarrassed)*: My, what?

OLDER: Your omb, your man.

FAIRLY YOUNG: O—my man—yes . . . how are you having yours?

OLDER: I'm having mine stewed because I like them that way, I think they're nicest when they're stewed.

FAIRLY YOUNG *(Doubtfully)*: I think they're nice that way too.

OLDER: Have yours any way you like, dear.

FAIRLY YOUNG: Yes . . . let me see. *(Pause)* I think I'll have mine boiled.

OLDER *(Interpreting)*: Voo donny ray poor mwah un omb stewed, a, poor moan ammy, un omb boiled.

HEADWAITER *(As before)*: Bien madame. Et comme boisson, madame?

OLDER: What do you want to drink, dear?

HEADWAITER *(Interpolating)*: Une bonne bouteille de champaigne, n'est-ce pas, madame?

FAIRLY YOUNG: I don't care.

OLDER: A voo donny ray, avek sellah, oon bootay der Ay-vyon.

HEADWAITER *(Almost bursting with rage)*: Merci mesdames. *(Turning to the waiting WAITER)* Bring two men immediately for these ladies and have one of the men boiled and the other stewed.

WAITER *(Saluting)*: Benissimo, sehr gut. *(He vanishes)*

OLDER *(Produces and opens a cigarettecase: offers it)*: Will you have a cigarette?

FAIRLY YOUNG *(Hastily, producing ditto)*: Try one of mine. They're camels.

OLDER: Thank you, I think I prefer lucky strikes. *(Each lights her own cigarette)* Well, dear. How do you like Paris?

FAIRLY YOUNG: I think Paris is darling. I've met so many people from New York.

OLDER: Yes, Paris is certainly cosmopolitan.

FAIRLY YOUNG: O, very.

OLDER *(After a pause)*: Have you been here long?

FAIRLY YOUNG: Only a few days. Dick and I arrived last—when was it—let me see: today is . . . Thursday. . . .

OLDER: Today is Tuesday.

FAIRLY YOUNG: Is today really Tuesday?

OLDER: Today must be Tuesday, because Monday was yesterday. I know, because yesterday I had a fitting on a dress I bought at Poiret's. You should see it—

FAIRLY YOUNG: O dear, then I missed an appointment at the hairdresser's if today is Tuesday. Well, I'll go tomorrow. . . . What were we talking about? I didn't mean to interrupt.

OLDER: Let me see . . . O I asked you if you'd been here long, that was it.

FAIRLY YOUNG: O yes, of course.—Why no, Dick and I arrived . . . last Friday, I guess it was—on the Aquitania.

OLDER: I came on the Olympic myself.

FAIRLY YOUNG: Really.

OLDER: Did you have a pleasant trip?

FAIRLY YOUNG *(Enthusiastically)*: Simply glorious. Dick was sick all the time.

OLDER: How silly of him. *(A pause)* I suppose you've been about a great deal since you arrived?

FAIRLY YOUNG: O yes. I've seen everything there is to see.

OLDER *(Dreamily)*: Have you seen that old church, such a beautiful old ruin, over somewhere to the East is it?

FAIRLY YOUNG *(Promptly)*: Which bank?

OLDER: I'm talking about a church, it's very famous, very old—

FAIRLY YOUNG: I meant which bank of the Sane is it on?

OLDER *(Unabashed)*: O, I don't know, but I think it was on the further one, if I remember rightly.

FAIRLY YOUNG: The interesting one where the students live?

OLDER: You know what I mean, the car tea a lat tan, and all that.

FAIRLY YOUNG: I think I know the one you mean.

OLDER: It's the right, isn't it? I'm always getting them mixed.

FAIRLY YOUNG: I never can keep them straight either.

OLDER: Well, anyway—it's the loveliest old thing—you must have seen it. *(Pause)*

FAIRLY YOUNG: If it's very old, I must have.

OLDER: O—it's very old! *(The women smoke. The whores and music snore. A pause.)* There was something I wanted to tell you, and it's completely gone out of my head. I can't think what . . . O, yes: this dress I've just bought. It's such a LOVELY dress.

FAIRLY YOUNG *(Insincerely)*: I should SO like to see it.

OLDER: We'll go around there tomorrow after lunch—it's black satin, very simple, but the loveliest lines you ever saw in your life, and just oceans of real Brussels lace. *(She makes an oceanic gesture)*

FAIRLY YOUNG: How wonderful. Did it cost much?

OLDER: I should say so—from Poiret, you know: terribly expensive . . . as I remember it, let me see: why I think I paid three of those very big notes; you know, the brown ones.

FAIRLY YOUNG: I thought the brown ones were fifty.

OLDER: The small brown ones are, but these were the big brown ones. *(A pause)*

FAIRLY YOUNG: The yellow ones with the pictures are a hundred, aren't they?

OLDER: Yes, the pictures are a hundred, and then there's a five hundred. The ones I was thinking of are the thousand, I guess—unless there's a ten-thousand franc note. . . . I always get confused whenever I try to figure out anything which has to do with money.

FAIRLY YOUNG: So do I, here. American money is so much more sensible, I should think they'd adopt it everywhere.

OLDER: Well, I suppose it would cause some difficulties.

FAIRLY YOUNG: You'd think they'd adopt it here, though. The French are supposed to be so intelligent.

OLDER *(Confidentially)*: O but they're not—really. Why, only today, I tried to make a taxidriver understand where I wanted to go: it was perfectly simple, song karawnt sank roo der lay twahl, and I said it over THREE times, and even then he couldn't seem to understand—

FAIRLY YOUNG: Yes. I know.

OLDER: —so finally I had to say it in English. And then he understood!

FAIRLY YOUNG: They seem to understand English better than French nearly everywhere in Paris, now.

OLDER: Well, I suppose it's the war, don't you think so?

FAIRLY YOUNG: Dick thinks so.

OLDER: Dick—?

FAIRLY YOUNG: My husband. He was in Paris during the war.

OLDER: O. Was he.

FAIRLY YOUNG: Yes. He started in by being a major, but he soon got promoted to colonel.

OLDER: How interesting. —I wonder if you know a man named Seward.

FAIRLY YOUNG *(Eagerly)*: Jim Seward or Jack Seward? I know them both well. I'm crazy about Jack. He came over on the boat with me.

OLDER: I think this one's name was Tom, or something like that. I can't quite remember. . . .

FAIRLY YOUNG *(As before)*: Is he blond and wonderful looking?

OLDER: No, he's rather dark, and very UNattractive: in fact, quite ugly.

FAIRLY YOUNG: O. *(A pause)*

OLDER: Tom Seward, yes that was his name. His father was a prominent banker or something.

FAIRLY YOUNG: I don't think I ever met him. *(A pause)* Why?

OLDER: O I just wondered. *(A long pause)*

FAIRLY YOUNG *(Glancing about her for the first time)*: It's quiet here, isn't it. I expected it to be lively.

OLDER: Did you?—I thought just the opposite. The name is so quiet: Pare Trank Eel. It means Tranquil Father, you know. *(A pause)*

FAIRLY YOUNG: I never heard of it. Is it well known?

OLDER: Only to those who KNOW. *(A pause)*

FAIRLY YOUNG: I was just thinking it looked very exclusive. *(The bell rings with terrific violence. Whores and music leap into consciousness. A MAN'S VOICE, cheerfully patronising, is heard in the vicinity of the doorway.)*

MAN'S VOICE: Here we are! *(In the doorway appear two WOMEN, one ELDERLY, one YOUTHFUL, attired in the last wail of fashion)*

ELDERLY *(Pushing YOUTHFUL)*: You go first, Alice.

YOUTHFUL *(Entering with a slouchy saunter which is intended to convey the impression that she is blasée, speaks in a flat Middle-western voice)*: So this is Paris. *(Stares about her, standing awkwardly and flatfootedly. The ELDERLY WOMAN follows, drawing herself up and using her lorgnette. Two men, alikelooking in evening dress, block the doorway.)*

OWNER OF MAN'S VOICE BEFOREMENTIONED: Go ahead, Will.

MAN ADDRESSED: You know the ropes, Bill. *(He sidesteps. BILL bursts into the room, followed by the HEADWAITER)*

HEADWAITER: Would you like a nice table sir, over here sir—. *(Salaaming, he rushes to a table in the corner opposite the GENTLEMAN and the BLOND GONZESSE. Pulls out chairs.)*

BILL: This all right for ever-body?

ELDERLY WOMAN *(Having completed her inspection of the room, smiles mysteriously)*: I think this will be all right.

BILL: Siddown ever-body. *(A* CHASSEUR *enters, taking off his cap, and approaches* WILL*)*

ELDERLY WOMAN: I'll sit here.

BILL: Thass right Lucy—where's Will?

YOUTHFUL WOMAN: Where do I go?

ELDERLY WOMAN: You sit here, Marjorie, where you can see everything.

WILL *(Who is standing, facing the* CHASSEUR *with an expression at once vague and mistrustful)*: How much do I give this feller, Bill?

YOUTHFUL WOMAN: There doesn't seem to be much to see.

BILL: Give 'im five francs. (WILL, *pulling out a wad of twenty, fifty and hundred franc notes from his trouser pocket, gives a fifty to the* CHASSEUR*)*

CHASSEUR *(Bowing briefly)*: Merci msieur. *(Putting on his cap he hurries out in search of new victims)*

ELDERLY WOMAN: Come here Will, and sit by me. *(A* VESTIAIRE *hurries in)*

HEADWAITER *(To the* WAITER, *who has been hiding respectfully behind his superior)*: Allez vite: cherchez-moi la carte. *(The* WAITER *sprints to a neighboring table, grabs a menu, returning hands it to the* HEADWAITER. *The* VESTIAIRE *comes up.)*

VESTIAIRE *(Insinuatingly)*: Voulez-vous vous débarasser msieurs mdames?

BILL: She wants our hats 'n' coats. *(He gives her his derby)*

ELDERLY WOMAN: I'll keep mine, it's rather chilly here.

BILL: Alice?

YOUTHFUL WOMAN: No thanks.

BILL *(To* VESTIAIRE*)*: Say too. *(The* VESTIAIRE *regretfully turns.* WILL *seizes her by the sleeve)*

WILL: Hay. *(Whispers)* Where's thuh. *(He gestures occultly, winking ponderously)*

VESTIAIRE *(Removing WILL'S derby from his hand)*: Par ici, msieur. *(She beckons: WILL follows her through the doorway)*

HEADWAITER *(Bending over BILL and holding the menu so that BILL cannot quite see it, speaks caressingly)*: Will you have a little soup sir, and some nice oysters—

BILL: Wait a minute. 'Re we all here? Where's—

HEADWAITER *(Apologetically, in a low voice)*: The gentleman'll be right in sir.

BILL: I getcha. *(Loudly)* Well now, what'd you girls like to eat?

ELDERLY WOMAN: You do the ordering, Billie dear, you know we can't read it.

HEADWAITER *(Suggestingly)*: Oysters are very nice sir, or a nice steak—

YOUTHFUL WOMAN *(Impatiently)*: I'll take anything.

BILL *(Importantly)*: Lessee. *(He takes the menu, studies it)*

HEADWAITER *(Coaxingly, almost playfully)*: A little soup to begin with sir—

BILL: Yes. Soup ahl un yon poor toolah mond.

HEADWAITER: Bien msieur.

ELDERLY WOMAN *(To YOUTHFUL WOMAN)*: Did you see those . . . *(She nods toward the whores)*

YOUTHFUL WOMAN: Uhhuh. *(She turns her dull gaze upon the BLOND GONZESSE. The BLOND GONZESSE fixes her with a glassy eye.)*

BILL: 'M ordering soup for Will.

ELDERLY WOMAN *(Quickly)*: That's right.

HEADWAITER: Et après. . . .

BILL: Ap ray, donny mwah daze weet.

HEADWAITER *(Approvingly)*: Des huitres, bien msieur. Quatre douzaines, n'est-ce pas msieur? *(WILL, hands in pockets, enters vaguely)*

ELDERLY WOMAN *(Beckoning anxiously)*: Over here, Will!

WILL *(Overhereing)*: Hullo everybody.

BILL *(Looks up)*: Siddown Will. Thought you fell overboard.

ELDERLY WOMAN: We ordered you some soup. *(WILL sits heavily beside her)*

HEADWAITER: Une douzaine chacun?

BILL: He wants to know how many—. *(Desperately to HEADWAITER)* We.

HEADWAITER *(Radiating approbation)*: Et pour la suite msieur—un bon rumstek—un chateau—un veau sauté—?

WILL *(Ponderously, growls)*: Thought I was lost out there.

ELDERLY WOMAN: Yes?

BILL: We we, kom voo voo lay. *(The HEADWAITER, beaming, writes down a great many things hurriedly on a pad)* Et ensuite—un peu de fromage—un dessert—you wish strawberries?

WILL: Got some pretty slick girls out there. One of 'em tried to get my watch.

BILL: Will you have strawberries?

YOUTHFUL WOMAN: All right, all right anything at all.

HEADWAITER: Strawberries very fresh.

BILL: Strawberries poor toola mond. Wutabout something to drink?

HEADWAITER: Il n'y a que champagne msieur.

BILL: We we, sham pain.

HEADWAITER *(Tears sheet from pad and hands it to WAITER, who mercurially disappears)* Bien messieurs mesdames. *(Turning, beckons vehemently to the music, which has stopped but which immediately recommences with redoubled vigor)*

OLDER WOMAN *(To FAIRLY YOUNG)*: I'll ask him.—May truh dough tell. *(The HEADWAITER wheels)* Seal voo play—*(He comes to her table)* Voo parlay onglay?

HEADWAITER *(Irritated)*: Yes, I speak English.

OLDER WOMAN *(Indicating WILL and BILL, whispers)*: Are those our ombs?

HEADWAITER: Yes madame. But they are not quite ready yet—a little patience, madame.

OLDER WOMAN: O, I see. All right. Thank you, may truh dough tell.

*(The* HEADWAITER *hurries off. The* OLDER *whispers the news to the* FAIRLY YOUNG, *who stares seductively at the ombs. Enter* HIM, *walking too straight, carrying in his left hand a cabbage. He walks too straight up to the table where the* BLOND GONZESSE *and the* GENTLEMAN *are sitting and bows interrogatively to the* GENTLE-MAN, *indicating an imaginary third place with a majestic wave of his right hand.)*

HIM: Permettez, monsieur?

BLOND GONZESSE *(Immediately)*: Oui monsieur. *(She giggles)*

GENTLEMAN: Sit down. *(*HIM *draws up a chair. Sits, with the cabbage in his lap.)* Waiter!

WAITER: Msieur?

HIM *(To* WAITER*)*: Trois whis-ky et une assiette.

WAITER: Une assiette msieur—comment—? Une assiette anglaise?

HIM *(Sternly)*: Non. Une assiette nature, pour le choux.

WAITER: Ah—pour le choux. Bien msieur. *(Exit)*

GENTLEMAN: I never forget faces.

HIM: Really?

GENTLEMAN: Your face is familiar.

HIM: Yes?

GENTLEMAN: I've seen you somewhere before.

HIM: Possibly. *(A pause)*

GENTLEMAN: Were you ever in a city where the money is called "poo"?

HIM: I may have been.

GENTLEMAN: I think you were, and I think that's where I met you.

HIM: The world's not so big, after all. *(The* BLOND GONZESSE *giggles)*

GENTLEMAN *(To* BLOND GONZESSE*)*: Pardon—meet my friend Mr.—

HIM *(Promptly)*: John Brown. *(Bows)*

BLOND GONZESSE: Enchantée, monsieur.

GENTLEMAN: Have a cigar. *(Producing two)* The lady prefers cigarettes.

HIM *(Taking one)*: Thanks. *(He and the* GENTLEMAN *bit off and spit out the tips of their cigars.* HIM *strikes a match: lights the* GENTLEMAN'S *cigar and his own.)*

GENTLEMAN *(Smoking)*: Did I understand you to say you were John Brown?

HIM *(Smoking)*: Correct.

GENTLEMAN: In that case let me ask you something: does your body lie mouldering in the grave? *(Leaning across the table)* Because mine does.

HIM: Yes?

GENTLEMAN: But that isn't all of it. *(Drawing himself up, remarks smilelessly)* My soul goes marching on. *(*HIM *inspects the cabbage gravely. The* BLOND GONZESSE *giggles.)* The lady doesn't believe me. She doesn't know who I am. I just met her.

HIM: Who are you?

GENTLEMAN: I am the unpublished photograph of George Washington crossing the Susquehanna in a breechesbuoy. Who are you.

HIM: I live here.

GENTLEMAN: In that case, let me ask you something: are you one of those God, damned, artists? *(The whiskies and a large plate arrive)*

WAITER *(To* HIM*)*: Voici msieur, l'assiette nature. *(The* BLOND GONZESSE *giggles)*

HIM *(Carefully transferring the cabbage from his lap to the empty plate and lifting carefully his whisky, answers)*: No. That is, not exactly: I earn money by taming jellyfish.

GENTLEMAN *(Picking up his whisky)*: The lady doesn't believe you. The lady doesn't believe anything.

HIM: The lady is a wise lady—à votre santé madame. *(Gravely bows to the* BLOND GONZESSE*)* Ashes to ashes. *(Bows gravely to the* GENTLEMAN*)*

GENTLEMAN: Ally upp. *(HIM and the* GENTLEMAN *drink their whiskies)*

YOUTHFUL WOMAN *(Angrily repulsing* BILL'S *half-hearted attempt to embrace her, and gazing rapturously at* HIM *who does not see her)*: Don't!

FAIRLY YOUNG WOMAN *(Excitedly whispers to* OLDER, *indicating* BILL*)*: I think mine's almost ready.

A WHORE *(Yawning, to a yawning whore)*: Rien à faire ce soir.

WILL *(Pouring himself his fourth glass of champagne and staring fixedly at the* OLDER WOMAN*)*: Some. Baby.

ELDERLY WOMAN *(To* WILL, *while desperately ogling the unnoticing* GENTLEMAN*)*: Give ME a little champagne, please.

GENTLEMAN *(To* HIM*)*: How much.

HIM: How much what?

GENTLEMAN: How much do you make?

HIM: O—thirty cents a jellyfish.

GENTLEMAN: What do you do with them, when they're tame?

HIM: I sell them to millionaires. *(He turns amorously to the* BLOND GONZESSE*)* Il fait chaud, n'est-ce pas, mademoiselle?

BLOND GONZESSE *(Amorously)*: Très chaud, monsieur.

GENTLEMAN *(To* HIM*)*: Been over here long?

HIM: Not very. *(He points to the cabbage)* I was born day before yesterday.

GENTLEMAN: In that case, you probably know a show I went to last night: foliz burshare. *(The* BLOND GONZESSE *giggles)*

HIM: Never heard of them.

GENTLEMAN: The lady doesn't believe I've been.—Waiter!

WAITER *(Who has just placed a third bottle of champagne on* WILL'S *table and a second bottle of Evian on the* OLDER WOMAN'S*)*: Msieur.

GENTLEMAN *(To* HIM*)*: The same? *(*HIM *nods)* Ong kore.

WAITER: La même chose—bien msieur. *(He sprints)*

OLDER WOMAN *(To* FAIRLY YOUNG, *pouring water in her glass)*: I don't remember ever being so thirsty.

GENTLEMAN *(To* HIM*)*: Are you married?

HIM: Sometimes.

GENTLEMAN: You ought to go to that show.

HIM: Good?

GENTLEMAN: Rotten. A bunch of amateurs and some hand-painted scenery. They don't know how to put on a show over here. Little Old New York is the only place where the theatre's any good. *(Two whiskies arrive)* One more whisky for the lady.

BLOND GONZESSE *(Protestingly)*: Non, merci.

HIM: The lady's got one. *(Indicates an untouched glass)*

GENTLEMAN: Give the lady a drink, waiter. Ong kore.

WAITER: Encore un wis-kee—bien msieur. *(Sprints)*

GENTLEMAN: As for the women, they're fat and they're clumsy and they're naked and they don't know they're alive. *(He drinks his whisky)* I can hand Paris only one thing: the Scotch is sure death. What are you doing with that cabbage? Taming it?

WAITER: Un wis-kee—voici msieur. *(Places another whiskey on the table)*

GENTLEMAN *(To* WAITER*)*: How much is all this?

WAITER: Ca vous fait. . . .

GENTLEMAN: Kom be an.

WAITER: Ca fait—quatre cent francs juste, msieur. *(The* BLOND GONZESSE *giggles)*

GENTLEMAN: The lady doesn't think I can pay for it. *(He produces a wallet and pulls out a five hundred franc note)* Sang song frong: keep the change. *(He puts back the wallet.)*

WAITER *(Turning white with pleasure)*: Merci msieur. *(He and the* BLOND GONZESSE *exchange significant glances)*

BILL *(Totally disregarding the anguish of the* ELDERLY WOMAN *who has been helping herself freely to champagne and is now sway-*

*ing dangerously against him, lifts his glass to the* FAIRLY YOUNG WOMAN*)*: Pyjama pyjama.

HIM *(Drinking his whisky, addresses the* GENTLEMAN*)*: Going back?

GENTLEMAN: Back?

HIM: Back to the dear old U.S.A.?

GENTLEMAN *(Drunkenly shaking his head)*: Can't do it.

HIM: No?

GENTLEMAN *(All of him leaning across the table speaks distinctly)*: Let me tell you something: I had a son. And he's a drunkard. And I had a daughter: and she's a whore. And my son is a member of all the best clubs in New York City. And my daughter married thirteen million dollars. And I'm a member of the God, damned, bourgeoisie. *(He passes out cold)*

HIM *(Solemnly, to the collapsed* GENTLEMAN*)*: Admitting that these dolls of because are dissimilar, since one goes up when the other comes down, and assuming a somewhat hypothetical sawhorse symmetrically situated with reference to the extremities of the strictly conjectural seesaw, god is the candlestick or answer. *(Arising, waves majestically to the music which immediately strikes up "Yes, We have No Bananas"—turning, bows to the* BLOND GONZESSE *who has just appropriated the* GENTLEMAN'S *wallet)* In that case, let me ask you something: shall we dance the I Touch? *(The* ELDERLY WOMAN *vomits copiously into* BILL'S *lap)*

## Scene IV

SCENE: *The three knitting rocking figures facing the picture with their backs to the audience.*

*The* DOCTOR'S *head has disappeared from the picture, leaving a black hole. The* WOMAN'S *head is in the picture; her eyes are closed.*

FIRST FIGURE: Terribly. Especially in summer.

SECOND: How simply frightful! All over them?

THIRD: Drowsiness rumblings sour risings heartburn water-brash and the feeling of being stuffed.

FIRST: That depends: sometimes.

SECOND: Is it very painful?

THIRD: Ask the man who owns one.

FIRST: Not very. Like falling down stairs, and you apply the same remedy—one stick of dynamite in a tumbler of ink before meals.

THIRD: Ask dad he knows.

SECOND: I understand the dynamite but what does the ink do?

THIRD: Comes out like a ribbon lies flat on the brush.

FIRST: Why the ink dissolves the guineapigs and makes them nervous.

SECOND: And what do they do after that?

THIRD: Look for the union label on every garment.

FIRST: They? Who?

SECOND: The guineapigs.

FIRST: O! They let go of the children.

SECOND: How time flies—you never know what to expect, do you.

*(The* WOMAN'S *head stirs in the picture: her eyes open slowly)*

FIRST: Yes life is a mystery at best.

THIRD: If it isn't an Eastman it isn't a Kodak.

SECOND: And we have so many things to be thankful for, haven't we.

*(The* DOCTOR'S *head appears in the picture)*

FIRST: I should say so: why my husband and I were married fifty years ago come day before yesterday and we've never had a single cross word—now what do you think of that?

DOCTOR'S HEAD *(Harshly, from the picture)*: If you wore your garters around your neck you'd change them oftener.

## Scene V

SCENE: *The room, still further revolved so that the fourth or invisible wall is the solid wall. The wall to the audience's right (corresponding to the solid wall of Scene I) is the mirror wall. The middle wall is the window wall. The door wall is to the audience's left. On the centre of the table, where* HIM'S *hat was lying at the beginning of Scene I, there is a vase of flowers.*

*ME and* HIM *sit, back to (or facing the same way as) the audience, at opposite ends of the sofa which is against the invisible wall.*

ME: I imagine, myself, it was very nice.

HIM: I remember morning. Silence. Houses in the river—April: the green Seine filled with houses, filled with windows out of which people look. And everything is upside down. . . . Then there comes a least breeze. And the people in the windows and the windows themselves and all the houses gradually aren't. I remember standing, thinking, in sunlight; and saying to myself "dying should be like this."

ME: Dying?

HIM: —To feel like one of the upsidedown people in one of the wrongsideup windows when a breeze comes.

ME *(After a pause)*: It must be a nice place, Paris, for a man.

HIM: I happened to be a dream there.

ME: But you're not any more. *(Suddenly)* Tell me, do I look very old?

HIM *(Smiles)*: How did you get that idea?

ME: Women don't get it, they're born with it. Besides—you told me, the first time I saw you again, that I'd changed.

HIM: I don't remember saying anything.

ME: You didn't know me—which is worse.

HIM: But that's asking too much of a dream.

ME: I expect I have changed *(Shudders slightly)*

HIM: Have I?

ME: Changed?—A little.

HIM: I ask because, if you remember, you once said you had changed but that I was the same.

ME: O—yes, I remember saying that. . . .

HIM: You were right about memories.

ME: Was I?

HIM: Wonderfully right.

ME: Isn't it queer. I feel as if we'd—as if you hadn't gone. . . . Do you feel that?

HIM: I can't believe that we're together.

ME: With me it's just the other way.

HIM: When one has been a dream, it takes some time to—. *(He gestures smoothly)*—So to speak, renovate oneself.

ME *(Almost to herself)*: Let's not talk about dreams any more.

HIM *(Looking at her)*: I shall try not to.

ME *(Taking his hand, smiles)*: Such a queer day, when I saw you again and you didn't recognize me—and I didn't care. *(A pause)*

HIM: It was raining.

ME: Terribly hard. When I saw you I was running, because I'd forgotten to take my umbrella. Then I stopped—

HIM: In the rain.

ME: —in front of you.

HIM: We looked at each other, probably.

ME: We never said anything.

HIM *(To himself)*: I seem to remember very well, looking.

ME: . . . Then you offered me your umbrella.

HIM: Did I?

ME: We walked along together under your umbrella. We walked quite a distance; and most of it, people were laughing.

HIM: Were people laughing?

ME: —Until we stood before the door. . . . Then I spoke to you. Do you remember what I said?—I said "it isn't raining." It hadn't been for some time and I knew; but I didn't say anything.

HIM: I didn't know.

ME: You must have been a little happy?

HIM: Yes.

ME: Then—do you know what you did?

HIM: No.

ME: Well, you shut the umbrella.

HIM: The key squeaked in the lock more than I expected. The floor creaked more than I remembered its creaking.

ME: Yes, I was going to use mine when you stopped me and took out yours.

HIM: You had forgotten giving me that key, once upon a time.

ME: I never dreamed you'd kept it.

HIM *(To himself)*: I couldn't go carefully enough.

ME: You frightened me a little when you shut the door. You shut it so very very gently. I remember how you walked to the sofa and how you sat down.

HIM: Perhaps I was afraid of breaking someone. *(A pause)*

ME: We sat for a long time, where we're sitting now.

HIM: A long time?

ME: Nearly an hour, I guess. Until you got up suddenly and looked out the window.

HIM: Outside, someone was putting away pieces of sky which looked remarkably like toys.

ME *(In a low voice)*: And always you stood, looking—. Your hands . . . folding, shutting. Finally (just as it was getting very dark)—"I think," you said "my hands have been asleep." Very gently you said that and went out, shutting the door carefully. I heard your feet going down the stairs. I sat, hearing for a long time in the rain your feet, in the dark. Walking. *(A pause)* Tell me—when you left, without your umbrella, where did you go?

HIM: "Go"?

ME: It's silly of me to ask—I ask because I want to. Did you go to a park . . . like the big one with the animals, or the little park where the harbor is?

HIM: Harbor—how did you guess? *(To himself)* Queer that I should have done that; avoiding the animals?

ME: Ships go out sometimes; maybe you were thinking of ships.

HIM: And sometimes come in. And there I met a man with green eyes . . .

ME: A man—? What was he doing?

HIM: Doing? Doing nothing, I think. Let me see: a man came and sat down beside me on a bench. Because it was raining.

ME: Or because he guessed you were lonely?

HIM: . . . and a crumpled hat; who said, I remember, that he had only just returned from Paris. O—and he didn't wear spats.

ME: Did he talk to you much?

HIM: I suppose so.

ME: What did he talk about—Paris?

HIM: Probably.

ME: Didn't you talk to him?

HIM: I don't think I did. O yes—no I didn't talk to him.

ME: Why?

HIM: Because I killed him.

ME *(Starting violently)*: —The man?

HIM: Himself.

ME: —You didn't—

HIM: Kill him?

ME: —him—

HIM: O, him. *(Easily)* Of course I didn't. *(Smiles)*—Just the other way 'round.

ME *(Earnestly)*: What do you mean?

HIM: It's clear now—can't you see? *(Gently)* He killed me.

ME: Please, dear, I'm—so nervous. *(Taking his other hand)* Don't.

HIM: —Frighten you? All right, sorry. He didn't kill me.

ME: Of course not!

HIM: On the contrary—instead, what did the wretch do?

ME: Never mind. Let's—

HIM: Why as sure as you live and as cool as you please producing from the vicinity of his exaggerated omphalos an automatic, he asked me to shoot himself; or perhaps I asked me to shoot himself, I can't quite remember which. . . .

ME: Why are you like this?

HIM: Or as I said to the man in the green hat with crumpled eyes: why in the name of Heaven should a gentleman recently returned from Paris ask him to kill myself? And do you know what the rascal replied to that?

ME: I don't want to know; let's talk about something else; the play.

HIM: —Sir, said he, the reason I ask me to kill yourself is that a gentleman also recently returned from Paris—

ME: The one you were working on when. The one, you know.

HIM: —from Paris, mind, has recently penetrated God's country by fast freight with the express purpose of—

ME: With the negroes in it.

HIM: —committing the pardonable sin with my ex . . . Libido, I think was the accurate and incredible word which he employed. *(Relaxing, looks upward)* Then the ocean, filled with trillions of nonillions of able-bodied seamen and only-half-human mermaids and thousands upon hundreds of whales, came up everywhere over the earth—up everywhere over the world—and up up up to the bench where we were sitting. And the mermaids' bellies were full of little slippery fish, and the frolicking great whales were swaying and playing upon harps of gold, and the seamen were sailing before the mast, and the ocean . . . the ocean rose and stood solemnly beside us, resting its chin in its hand and looking at the recently returned gentleman from Paris. Whereupon the recently returned gentleman from Paris invited the ocean to sit down.

ME: You—

HIM: But You never said anything. You was much too busy, eyeing the mermaids and counting the seamen and admiring the golden harps of the most enormous of all mammals—

ME: —didn't—

HIM: —until suddenly You looked. *(He smiles)* The ocean had gone: and away off—ever so many thousands of hundreds of billions of millions of years away—You heard a sound. It was the sound of the mermaids, with bellies full of gooey fish and with long hair, chasing the seamen everywhere and snatching the golden harps from the hands of the resplendent whales. And all this sound went away slowly. Finally You looked all about You: and You was alone, holding in You's hand—. *(He laughs)*—A papyrus from Harun-al-Rashid inviting us all to petit dejeuner in the most excellent Arabic at twenty-three hours on January thirty-second, seven thousand one hundred and seventeen Columbus cross the ocean blue. *(A pause)*

ME *(Quietly)*: Is that all?

HIM: I put it in my pocket—the ocean green. But You didn't care a continental damn.

ME: That's all?

HIM *(Nodding in the direction of the table, upstage)*: I see flowers.

ME: Yes, thank you. *(A pause)* Do you know something?

HIM: I understand less and less.

ME: You have changed.

HIM: Much?

ME: Quite a lot: your eyes . . . or maybe it's the light. Did you—

HIM: Aren't my eyes green?

ME: It's been a long time, hasn't it; since you—. *(Timidly)* Please tell me. Am I different . . . very much?

HIM: "Different"?

ME: Olderlooking.

HIM *(Smiles)*: You seem to me a little younger, just a little younger.

ME: You're joking. I know I look older. *(Shudders)*

HIM: I'm not joking, seriously. —So my eyes have changed. Probably you're right. Like Rip Van Winkle they've been asleep.

ME: You mean that when your eyes see me they know they've been asleep.

HIM: I really mean that they don't have people like you, up there.

ME: Where?

HIM: Up in the mountains where they play a game with thunder. Anywhere. Nowhere. Where for a hundred years I fell asleep.

ME: O—those mountains.

HIM: Those.

ME *(After a pause)*: Are you quite sure you're not sorry that you're awake?

HIM: Wonderfully sure—you see, Rip's story and my story are . . . different.

ME *(Laughing)*: Because you haven't a beard?—O but I'm glad you haven't a beard. You know I can't stand men with beards. Or spats.

HIM: Not because I haven't a beard, but because when I woke up and came down out of those mountains, you were younger than before.

ME: How do you know that I. Maybe I'm married, and have ever so many . . . didn't his?

HIM: His?

ME: Rip Van Winkle's girl; or was it his wife? I thought she'd forgotten all about him in the meantime and married someone else.

HIM *(Thoughtfully)*: I only seem to remember that she was dead.

ME: O. . . .

HIM *(Vaguely)*: I was thinking . . . so am I. I suppose nobody, including his children, really believed him when he told them.

ME: When he told them—about the mountains?

HIM: About the mountains and about being asleep.

ME: Do you think? O dear; I'm sorry, but this is getting too complicated for me.

HIM *(Earnestly)*: Please be happy. Why should I talk about myself? I'd much rather talk about you.

ME: Me? *(Bitterly)* There's nothing to talk about.

HIM: Isn't there? I'm very sorry. We all make mistakes.

ME *(Looks at him)*: I know. I make them.

HIM: You? Stop.

ME: Listen. Suppose—

HIM: Don't suppose.

ME *(Bravely)*: —suppose I made a mistake; and it was the mistake of my life. And suppose: O suppose—I'm making it!

HIM *(Steadily)*: You're wrong, quite wrong. It's the mistake of my life.

ME *(Whispers)*: Is it?

HIM *(Quietly)*: Yes.

ME *(Looking at him)*: It may take two people to make a really beautiful mistake.

HIM *(Expressionlessly)*: The nicest things happen by themselves.— Which reminds me: I had a dream only the other day. A very queer dream: may I tell it to you? *(A pause)*

ME: Do you want to very much?

HIM: If you don't very much mind.

ME *(Hesitantly)*: If it's not too queer.

HIM: Will you promise to interrupt me if it's too queer?

ME: All right.

HIM *(Leaning forward, looks at nothing)*: You were with me in a sort of room. I was standing beside you and you seemed to be telling me something. But I was only tremendously glad to feel you so near. . . .

ME: Go on.

HIM: That was beautiful to me.—Then you took my left hand and you led me somewhere else in this room—and through the roomshaped dark softness I tiptoed wadingly. You paused and I stood next you: next your blood, your hair, hands, breathing. I felt that you were smiling a little. You pointed to something. And stooping carefully I could not quite see—but through this dark softness I seemed to feel—another person, lying very quietly with an entire quietness that queerly frightened me. . . . May I go on?

ME: Go on.

HIM: When I could see, this other person's eyes and my eyes were looking at each other. Hers were big and new in the darkness. They seemed to be looking at me as if we had known each other somewhere else. They were very close—so close that my breath almost touched them: so close that my mind almost touched what looked at me from them . . . I can't describe it—a shyness, more shy than you can ever imagine, a shyness inhabiting very easily and very skillfully everything which is profoundly fragile and everything which we really are and everything which we never quite live. But—just as I almost touched this shyness—it suddenly seemed to touch me; and, touching, to believe me and all from which I had come and into which I was changing with every least thought or with each carefully hurrying instant. I felt a slight inexplicable gesture—nearer than anything, nearer than my own body—an inscrutable timidity, capturing the mere present in a perfect dream or wish or Now . . . a peering frailness, perfectly curious about me; curiously and perfectly created out of my own hope and out of my own fear. . . . I did not see any more, then. *(Pauses; smiling, resumes)* Then I stooped a little lower and kissed her hair with my lips and with the trembling lips of my mind I kissed her head, herself, her silence. But as I kissed her, she seemed to me to be made out of silence by whatever is most perfectly silent; so that, to find out if she were perhaps real, I spoke to her—and her voice answered as if perhaps not speaking to me at all, or as if it felt embarrassed because it knew that it was doing something which it should not do; and yet, I remember her voice was glad to feel, close by it, the unreal someone whom I had been.—Then the darkness seemed to open: I know what I saw then: it was a piece of myself, a child in a crib, lying very quietly with her head in the middle of a biggish pillow, with her hands out of the blankets and crossing very quietly and with a doll in the keeping fingers of each hand. . . . So you and I together went out of this opened darkness where a part of ourselves somehow seemed to be lying—where something which had happened to us lay awake and in the softness held a girl doll and a boy doll. Perhaps you closed the door, gently . . . but I remember nothing about coming into the light. *(His eyes search the face of* ME *and find a different nothing)* That is my dream. *(Rises)* Into the mirror with it, we'll throw it away! *(Strides to the mirror, makes a quick futile gesture and stands facing the mirror. A short pause.* ME *rises and goes to* HIM *slowly: stands, simply, sorrowfully. Turning from the mirror to* ME, HIM *speaks slowly.)* Hark. That was my dream which just fell into my soul and broke.

ME *(Touches his arm pityingly, slightly)*: I guess it took so long to fall because it was made of nothing. *(She returns to the sofa and sits down)*

HIM: You have a bright idea. *(Returning to the sofa, sits opposite her. A pause.)* Shall we smoke a cigarette—or two perhaps? *(Fumbles*

*in pockets, finds matches and a package of cigarettes: offers ciga-*
*rettes to* ME *who does not see them)* Then I will; unless you. . . .

ME: I don't mind.

HIM *(Lights carefully his cigarette: pockets the matchbox. Presently*
*remarks to himself.)*: But there was a dog, named something or
other. *(Short silence)*

ME: A dog.

HIM: I used to take him to bed with me. In fact we traveled everywhere together. God spelled backwards.

ME: What sort of a dog?

HIM: The name being Gipsy. It didn't last long because it was a cloth
dog. Tell me something.

ME: What.

HIM *(Quietly)*: Tell me you used to have a cloth dog too.

ME: I didn't . . . at least I don't think so.

HIM: Didn't you? Not ever? There was a battleship, which wound
up, with invisible wheels that made it move along the floor: it
was very fragile. They called it The Renown.—Did you have
dolls?

ME: I guess so, I don't remember.

HIM: I perfectly remember that I had a great many dolls, but that I
only loved one—a wax doll named Bellissima who melted in
front of the fire. *(Getting up, strolls to the table)*

ME *(Half to herself)*: I suppose you cried.

HIM: On the contrary, I asked for a cup of tea. *(He takes from the*
*table an imaginary cup and saucer; drops into the imaginary cup*
*an imaginary piece of sugar)*—But you have given me symbols.
Look: I see my life melting as what you call Winter. . . . The
edges are fading: gradually, very gradually, it diminishes. *(Takes*
*an imaginary sip)* But notice: there there is a purpose in the accident, I mean there is someone beyond and outside what hap-

pens—someone who is thirsty and tired. Someone, to whom the disappearance of my being sweetens unbeing as, let us say, this dissolving cube of sugar—pardon: God would like a slice of lemon. *(Takes an imaginary slice)* Thank you. We are all of us just a trifle crazy, aren't we? Like Archimedes with his mirrors and like old Mr. Benjamin F. who flew kites in a thunderstorm, which reminds me—I never told you that I was flying a kite. And it pulled and rose: wonderfully reaching out and steadily climbing, climbing over the whole world until you'd never believe anything in your life could be so awfully far and bright—until you almost thought it had found some spot where Spring is all the time. . . . But suddenly my foolish hands were full of common on twine string.

ME *(Looking straight before her, speaks to herself after a moment)*: It's snowing.

HIM: Gay may change, but all my thoughts are in the wash and I haven't a clean thing to put on. —After all, thoughts are like anything else you wear, they must be sent to the crazy laundry once in a while and the crazy laundry wears out more crazy thoughts than ever a crazy man did. Hypnos and Thanatos, a couple of Greek boys who made a fortune overnight, the laundry of the Awake, Incorporated: having mangled our lives with memories it rinses them in nightmare. *(A drum sounds faintly. ME starts.)* I think I hear nothing. *(Puts imaginary tea carefully on table; turns, slowly walks to the middle of the room and stands facing the audience)* But If I ask you something, now, will you promise to answer truthfully? *(She shakes her head)* Because you can't? —Tell me; why can't you answer me truthfully, now?

ME *(Rising)*: Now you want—truth?

HIM: With all my life: yes!

ME *(Advancing toward him slowly)*: You wanted beauty once.

HIM *(Brokenly)*: I believed that they were the same.

ME: You don't think so any longer?

HIM: I shall never believe that again.

ME *(Pauses, standing before him)*: What will you believe?

HIM *(Bitterly)*: That beauty has shut me from truth; that beauty has walls—is like this room, in which we are together for the last time, whose walls shut us from everything outside.

ME: If what you are looking for is not here, why don't you go where it is? *(The drumsound heightens)*

HIM: In all directions I cannot move. Through you I have made a discovery: you have shown me something . . . something about which I am doubtful deep in my heart. I cannot feel that everything has been a mistake—that I have inhabited an illusion with you merely to escape from reality and the knowledge of ourselves. *(To himself)* How should what is desirable shut us entirely from what is? No! That must be not quite all: I will not think that the tragedy can be so simple. There must be something else: I believe that there IS something else: and my heart tells me that unless I discover this now I will never discover it. —Am I wrong?

ME: You were talking about dolls. You see, I think sometimes.

HIM: Are you thinking, now?

ME: Now—yes. *(Total darkness. The drumsound drowns in a whirling nearness of mingling voices out of which juts suddenly ONE VOICE.)*

ONE VOICE: Ladies un genlmun right dis way step dis way evrybudy tuh duh Princess Anankay tuh duh Tatood Man tuh duh Huemun Needl tuh duh Missin Link tuh duh Queen uv Soipunts tuh duh Nine Foot Giun tuh duh Eighteen Inch Lady tuh duh Six Hundud Pouns uv Passionut Pullcrytood tuh duh Kink uv Borneo dut eats ee-lectrick light bulbs!

## Scene VI

SCENE: *The stage has become a semicircular piece of depth crowded with jabbering and gesticulating people, viz.* HIM *(hatted), the other participants in Act 2 with the exception of those characters which were played by the* DOCTOR, *and the three* MISS WEIRDS *minus their chairs and knitting. The circumference of the semicircle is punctuated at equal intervals by nine similar platforms. The fifth platform (counting, from either extremity of the circumference, inward) supports a diminutive room or booth whose front wall is a curtain. On each of the other eight platforms sits lollingly a freak.*

*Beginning with the outermost platform to the audience's left and following the circumference of the semicircle inward we have:* NINE FOOT GIANT, QUEEN OF SERPENTS, HUMAN NEEDLE, MISSING LINK *and the fifth or inmost platform with its mysterious booth. Continuing, outward, we have:* TATOOED MAN, SIX HUNDRED POUNDS OF PASSIONATE PULCHRITUDE, KING OF BORNEO *and, on the outermost platform to the audience's right,* EIGHTEEN INCH LADY.

MISS STOP WEIRD *(To* MISS LOOK*)*: I don't suppose he really eats them. *(To* MISS LISTEN*)* Do you? *(All three* WEIRDS *shake their mask-faces skeptically)*

HIM *(Bowing and removing his battered hat)*: Excuse me, ladies—. *(Indicates the* DOCTOR, *who, disguised as a hunchback* BARKER, *has just appeared on the platform of the* GIANT*)*—Who is that little creature?

MISS STOP: A harmless magician with whom we are only slightly acquainted.

MISS LOOK: A master of illusion.

MISS LISTEN: A person of no importance, his name is Nascitur.

HIM *(Bows and replaces his battered hat on his head: looking about him, speaks to himself)*: Barnum, thou shouldst be Darwin at this hour.

BARKER *(Beckons fervently from the platform of the rising* NINE FOOT GIANT, *toward whom the crowd swirls)*: Make it quick goils kummun fellurs foist we have, Dick duh Giunt I begs tuh call duh undievieded attention uv all lilypewshuns here presun tuh dis unparrallul phenomenun uv our own day un time duh leas skepticul may be pardun fur nut believin wut I states us duh in-con-tro-voituble troot dut dis extraordinury freak uv nachure wen standin in his stockin feet describes uh longitoodinul trajectury uv one hundun un eight inches no more no less in duh gigantic palm uv his colussul han he easily supports his lidl frien Madame Petite while ut duh same time consultin uh twentytwo carut gole timepiece made tuh ordur by uh famous Swiss consoin duh diul uv wich measures fourteen inches in dieametur un is protected by windowglass one quartur uv un inch in tickness upun duh summit uv his ee-normous head he wears uh speciully constructed strawhat weighin five pouns un fourteen ounces duh amount uv clawt require fur uh single pair uv dis poisun's elephantine pants would make six blokes like youse un me two un one half suits apiece his mammut neddur extremities fur wich numbur twenty-six shoes has been created bohs toiteen toes all in poific condition duh smalles biggur dun my wrist expoits have decided upon investigation dut in duh course uv one loonur day his garganchoon appetite consumes un duh average frum toitytwo tuh fortyfive ordinury beefsteaks ur duh protein ee-quivalunt it is estimated by duh managemunt uv dis exhibit dut twelve normul poisuns could exis fur fiftyfour hours twentytree minutes nine un sevuneights secuns un wut dis monstur communly annihilates fur breakfust alone I will merely add dut in ordur tuh facilitate inspection uv oit's mohs vas biped uh sixteen hundud candlepowur rubburtire telescope is placed ut duh disposition uv duh genrul public fur wich no extruh charge will be made walk right up un bring duh chilrun. *(He steps down and disappears in the crowd.* The GIANT *displays his watch, converses, offers photographs of himself. Many grasp the opportunity to observe him through the telescope. The* BARKER, *reappearing on the platform of the* EIGHTEEN INCH LADY, *beckons fervently.)* Dis way gents step dis way ladies—. *(The crowd swirls in his direction)*—Nex we have, Madame Suzette Yvonne Hortense Jacqueline Heloise Petite duh eighteen inch Parisiun doll un uncompromisin opticul inspection uv dis lidl lady will prove tuh duh satisfaction uv all consoin dut dis lidl lady is uh poificly form pocket edition uv sheek femininity born undur duh shadow uv duh Eyfl Towur in Paris were she buys all her close spiks floounly nineteen languages excloosive uv her native tongue is toityone years old in duh course uv her adventurous career has visited each un evry country uv duh civilised un uncivilise globe incloodin Soviet Russiuh were subsequunt tuh bein arrested by duh Checkur us uh spy she wus kidnapped un kep fur sevuntytwo hours widout food ur drink in duh inside ovurcoat pocket uv uh membur uv duh Secret Soivice havin escape by cuttin her way out wid uh pair uv nailscissurs she fell tuh duh frozun ground in uh dead faint in wich she wuz discovur by uh faitful moocheek who fled wid her across duh steps uv Siberiuh pursood by wolves un suckseeded in deliverin her tuh duh French consul ut duh Polish frun-teer receivin us uh reward fur his valur frum duh French guvurnmunt duh crorduhgair wid two palms un frum duh Polish ortorities duh cross uv Sain Graballsky wile duh lidl lady hoiself presented her rescoor wid un autograph photo in spite uv her wellestablish Parisiun origin Madame Petite is passionutly fond uv duh home wus in fac sevun times married tuh various internationully famous specimuns uv duh uppercrust uv duh pigmy woild such us Purfessur Tom Tumb un has divorced ur outlived all her husbans us uh mewzishun Madame is equully voisitil purfurrin especiully duh French horn trombone xylophone violin granpieannur youkuhlayly un jewshap un wich insturmunts she has had duh honur tuh purform before duh crown heads uv five nations un tree continunts duh genrul public will be gratifie tuh loin dut Madame Suzette Yvonne Hortense Jaqueline Heloise Petite has recunly completed duh only autentic story uv her life wich undur duh significunt title Minyuhchoors uv Romance ur Many Abelards has already sold out four editions uv one hundud tousund copies each un is ut presun in duh process uv bein tran-slated intuh twenty languages incloodin Arabic un Eskimo Madame Petite will be glad tuh answur any un all questions un give advice tuh duh best uv her ability un all un any subjects tuh whoever cares tuh unboidun her ur his troubles male un female step right up.

MISS LOOK WEIRD *(Suspiciously)*: What was she doing among the Bolsheviki?

BARKER: I will answur dut unnecessury question Madame Petite wus un uh mission uv moicy havin been delegated by duh French Red Cross tuh assis duh Salvation Army in its uplif woik among starvin Armeniun chilrun nooly rescood frum duh Toiks in West Centrul Youkraniuh.

MISS LOOK WEIRD *(Satisfied)*: Thank you. *(The* EIGHTEEN INCH LADY *converses and offers copies of her book and photographs of herself. The* BARKER *disappears, only to reappear on the* QUEEN OF SERPENTS' *platform.)*

BARKER *(Beckoning fervently to the crowd)*: Dis way ladies ovur here gents—. *(The crowd swirls in the direction of the* QUEEN OF SERPENTS, *who rises)*—Get uh knockdown tuh Herpo chawms duh lawges specimuns uv duh reptillyun genus each un evry one alive dis way fellurs take uh good squint ut Herpo hanuls duh deadlies becaws mohs poisunous uv all snakes duh cobruh duh capello like youse boys would hanul yur bes goil ovur here evrybudy see duh only livin boaconstrictur in captivity lengt toitynine feet sevun un nine toitysecunds inches swollud five indigenes ten cartridge belts six Winchestur rifles fortytwo rouns uv amyounition un uh Stetson hat ut one gulp subsequunly capchoord wile fast asleep by Capn Frank Mac Dermot D.S.C. etceteruh un shipped F.O.B. un twelve freightcars fur twentyone days tuh duh mowt uv duh Amazon rivur nevur woked up till fiftyfour hours out tuh sea wen duh en-tire crew incloodin duh capn took toins settin un duh heavily-padlock covur uv duh fortyfive foot bamboo box boun wid steel hoops in wich duh monstur wus tempurrurrilly imprisoned in spite uv wich precaution he trashed about so much duh S.O.L. passengurs wus all seasick till duh ship reached Hamburg were sevun uv um died see duh mammut rep-tile wine hisself lovinly toiteen times aroun Herpo wile she drinks un ice-cream soduh un smokes Virginiuh cigarettes dis way ladies un gents dis way. *(Steps down and disappears in the crowd. The* QUEEN OF SER-PENTS *takes out of a box, wraps around her and puts back in the box, four ancient and decrepit snakes, each larger than the other.)*

VIRGO OF ACT, TWO, SCENE 2 *(Fascinated)*: I hate snakes—ugh!

QUEEN OF SERPENTS *(Calmly, through her gum)*: Dat's because youse cawn't chawm dum dearie. *(Laughter)*

BARKER *(Reappearing on the platform of the* KING OF BORNEO, *who rises)*: Evrybudy dis way—. *(He gestures fervently. The crowd swirls toward the* KING OF BORNEO.*)* —Nex we comes tuh one uv duh principul kyouriosities uv dis ur any epock sometimes frivolously allooded tuh by ignorun poisuns us Duh Huemun Ostrich I refois propurly speakin tuh His Impeereel Majusty Kakos Kalos duh ex-Kink uv Borneo duh lad wid duh unpunkshooruble stumick speciully engaged ut ee-normous expense fur duh benefit uv duh Great Americun Public durin uh recen revolooshun in purhaps duh mohs primitive uv all semicivilise commyounities King Kakos Kalos nut only los his trone but had duh additionul misforchoon tuh be trode by his noomerous enemies intuh uh dun-john ur hole tuh use duh vulgur woid approximutly ninety six feet in dept un twotoids full uv rainwatur frum wich he wus pulled aftur fourteen days un nights un forcibly fed nails tincans broken glass barbwire un uddur dangerous objecs ovur uh period uv toitysix hours ut duh end uv wich time duh revolooshunuries lef dier victim fur dead but nix kid fur tanks tuh duh kink's younique un unparllul constitution wich us any uv youse is ut liburty tuh ascertain can assimilut wid ease such hidertoo erroneously considured indiegestubl substunces us carpettacks knittinneedles safety razorblades pins jackknives un dynamite he live tuh tell uh tale so incredible us tuh outrivul duh imaginury experiunces uv duh Barun Munchchowsun hisself but whose vuracity is prove beyon duh shadow uv uh doubt by duh fac dut it bein now five tuh five ur teatime in one two tree four five minutes Kink Kakos Kalos may be seen by all presun in duh intimut act uv swallurin un ee-lectrick light bulb step right up ladies un gents Duh Huemun Ostrich is in duh tent duh Kink's waitin fur youse KRK KRK KRK he champchomps sharp un brittle chews bright prickly glass. *(Disappears in the crowd. The* KING OF BORNEO *holds up a huge electric light bulb, points to it, points to his mouth and winks solemnly to the spectators.)*

FIRST FAIRY OF ACT TWO, SCENE 8 *(Soprano)*: How unpleasant.

SECOND FAIRY OF DITTO *(Alto)*: Positively repellent.

THIRD FAIRY OF DITTO: Perfectly disgusting.

FOURTH FAIRY OF DITTO: Makes one absolutely nauseated—ugh!

KING OF BORNEO *(Furiously)*: Sempre abasso Savoia putana madonna viva Lenine! *(He crams the electric light bulb far into his mouth— chews noisily. The* FOURTH FAIRY *faints and is carried off by the other three* FAIRIES.*)*

BARKER *(Reappearing on the platform of the* HUMAN NEEDLE*)*: Right dis way evrybudy—. *(He beckons fervently. The crowd swirls toward the* HUMAN NEEDLE, *who rises.)*—Nex we have, Adamus Jones fumilyully known tuh his many friens us Duh Huemun Needl dis young man is twentytree years old un still lookin fur uh wife summuh youse ladies in duh same interestin condition bettur tink twice before toinin down his-----statistics reinforce wid copious affidavits tens tuh show dut Mr. Jones who is uh native uv Melbourne Australiuh is sevunty un tree quarters inches in height un sevun un one eight inches in widt no more no less his highly illoominatin story is us follows ut duh age uv toiteen years Mr. Jones weighed approximutly tree hundud pouns un wus un acute suffrur frum many uv duh besknown ailmunts such us noomoniuh gout acne tootache indiegestion pulmunnurry tooburcyoulosis un dut mohs obscoor uv all huemun diseases cindurulluh in considuration uv wich fact uh council made up uv mohs uv duh notuble soigeons un speciulis frum duh Younighted Kinkdumb requested duh suffrur tuh place hisself upun uh carefully selected gastrunomic progrum compose chiefly uv watur radishes stringbeans un wustursheer sauce upun wich he has subsisted evur since ut duh presun writin Mr. Jones tips duh beam ut precisely sixtynine pouns un says he nevur felt bettur in his life wears day un night un his left ankle chust above duh knee un ordinury size sealring inscribe wid duh initiuls A.J. un presunted tuh duh wearur un duh fort uv Chooleye nineteen hundud un five by duh Inturnationul An-tie-hippo-fajic Association in tribute tuh his undenieubl poisyveerunce loyalty un courage dis way evrybudy step dis way. *(Disappears. The* HUMAN NEEDLE *converses, offers photographs of himself and displays his anklering.)*

MISS LOOK WEIRD *(To* MISS LISTEN*)*: Think of a man starving himself to avoid honest labour! *(*MISS LISTEN *shakes her maskface disgustedly)*

BARKER *(From the platform of the rising* SIX HUNDRED POUNDS OF PASSIONATE PULCHRITUDE, *gestures fervently)*: All right boys un goils right ovur here un make it snappy—. *(The crowd swirls toward him)*—Nex we have, upun uh speciully design reinforce concrete platform wich travuls wid her werever she goes duh knee plus ultry uv affectionut obesity duh indolunt acmy uv amorous adiposity duh mountain uv libidinous eequilibrium Miss Eva Smith bettur known tuh un legiun uv admirurs us Lidl Eva built like uh big bright bunch uv B. U. tiful bulloons takes one minute un sevunteen secuns fur all uv um tuh sit down two minutes un fiftytwo secuns fur all uv um tuh stand up un frum half uh day tuh twentyfour hours fur duh on-sombul tuh rise from uh recumbunt position unassisted by duh stopwatch ladies un genlmun tuh contumplate dis climax uv frankly female corpulanse is tuh agree wid duh celubrated preachur who wus hoid tuh remark diereckly aftur makin Lidl Eva's acquantunce dut if duh o-riginul Eve had been like her duh price uv figleaves would have tripled in duh Gawdn uv Eden step right up close evrybudy youse nevur seen nutn like Eva caws Eva doan begin un Eva doan end un Eva's chust one chin aftur unuddur dis way ladies blow yur eyes tuh uh good time wid duh livin illustration uv duh famous maxim Eat Un Grow Tin I wishes tuh announce in duh case uv Miss Smith dut duh managemunt inkois no responsubility fur feyenanciul un uddur losses occasion tuh poisuns nut already acquainted wid duh fac dut youse can lose uh five dollur bill in duh smalles wrinkle uv her eyelid step right up glimpse duh six hundud pouns of poisunully conducted pullcrytood dut makes uh billiardball look like uh cookie dis way tuh duh fort diemension. *(The* SIX HUNDRED POUNDS OF PASSIONATE PULCHRITUDE *converses and offers photographs of herself as the* BARKER *disappears in the crowd)*

MISS LISTEN WEIRD *(To* MISS LOOK*):* You'd think people would have a little shame, wouldn't you. *(*MISS LOOK *shakes her mask face disgustedly)*

BARKER *(From the* MISSING LINK'S *platform)*: Ladies un genlmun—. *(The crowd swirls toward his fervent beckonings: the* MISSING LINK *does not move)*—Gimme duh honur uv yur attention nex we have, Ge Ge duh mystury uv duh ages duh missin link in duh chain uv evulooshun frum prehistoric times tuh now duh huemun inturrogationpoint duh secrut uv our hairy ancesturs nut tuh be confuse wid manifole mendacities fakes counterfeit ur spyourious imitations uv duh o-riginul wich wus discovered in nineteen hundud un one in duh jungles uv Darkest Africuh by un expedition compriesin toiteen memburs uv duh Royul Darwiniun Society see It pounce upun Its meat like summuh youse fellurs seen uh swell skoit pounce on uh T. totully transparunt bargain ut duh lonjuhray countur eminun speciulis frum all ovur dese You-nighted States un purfessurs uv sighkology uv our foremost universities havin toroughly examine Ge Ge by evry intimut means known tuh duh corporeel un mentul sciences incloodin syntetic bloodtests telepatic waves cerebrul photogruphy postprandiul iodic injections testicullur hypnotism rhapsodic vaginul eelectrolysis decalcomaniuh un X ray have purnounce Him ur Her posolutely younique un absitively jenyouwine five hundud dollars reward will be paid tuh duh man womun ur chile dut can solve Ge Ge's mystury step dis way evrybudy. *(Disappears, as the* MISSING LINK *jumps about uttering uncouth cries and pointing happily to* ITSELF*)*

WILL AND BILL OF ACT TWO, SCENE 4 *(In unison, to the* MISSING LINK*)*: Who are you?

MISSING LINK *(Interrupting Its antics, haughtily retorts in excellent English)*: I am. *(It resumes Its crying and jumping)*

BARKER: Right ovur here ladies dis way gents step right up evrybudy—. *(The crowd swirls toward the platform of the* TATTOOED MAN, *who rises)*—Ladies un genlmun nex we have, E. I. Dolon duh Tatood Man born in duh city uv Boston un duh twelft day uv Augus eighteen hundud un ninetyeight shipped us cabinboy un duh skoonur Muddur Mucree chust off duh coast uv Timbucktoo duh vessul hit uh cyclone un sunk in midocean all hans bein lost excep duh heroic cabinboy who swum fur sevun days un six nights landin in uh state uv complete spirichool un physicul exhustion only tuh fine hisself surrounded by uh tribe uv two hunded headhuntin maneatin canibuls all polygamous starknaked un yellin bloody moidur wus ovurpowured in spite uv un heroic defence un put in duh fatninpen fur Sunday dinnur in wich pitiful condition he nevurduhless suckseeded in attractin duh notice uv duh favorite wife uv duh canibul kink who had him released un made uh membur uv duh tribe un condition dut his en-tire body widout exception should be adorned embellished un uddurwise ornamented wid emblems mottos pickshurs un similur insigniuh symbolic uv duh occasion prefurin decoration tuh det duh heroic seamun ak Y. essed wid duh trooly incredibul results wich fur duh fois time it is duh privilege uv duh genrul public tuh behold incloodin un soitn more intimut parts uv Mr. Dolon's unatumy portraits uv his toityfive B. U. tiful wives all between duh ages uv twelve un sixteen step right up ladies un gents.

MISS STOP WEIRD *(Skeptically)*: May I ask how long this person lived among the savages?

BARKER: Youse may lady fur ten years durin wich time E. I. Dolon

convoited duh en-tire tribe tuh Christianity un in addition estab-
lished uh tuh speak mily flourishin branch uv duh Y.W.C.A.

MISS STOP WEIRD (*Convinced*): That was very noble of him. (*The*
BARKER *steps down from the* TATTOOED MAN'S *platform and
disappears in the crowd. The* TATTOOED MAN *revolves slowly.*)

ENGLISHMAN OF ACT TWO, SCENE 6: I say old egg, you carry a bally
picture-gallery on your back—what?

TOTTOOED MAN (*Insultedly*): Dat ain no picher gallry, buddie.

ENGLISHMAN: Indeed? I rather supposed it was.

TATTOOED MAN (*Indignantly*): Soitnly not. Dat's Awt, dat is.

BARKER (*Reappearing beside the fifth platform, gestures fervently and
shouts*): Evrybudy dis way please—. (*The crowd swirls toward
the fifth platform with its mysterious curtained booth*)—Now we
comes tuh duh cornbeefuncaviare uv duh hole shebang duh
boin my close I'm in Heavun duh now youse sees it un now
youse tinks youse sees it duh jenyouwine P.S. duh resistunce duh
undielooted o-riginul milkshake uv duh ages Princess Anankay duh woil's foist un foremohs exponent uv yaki-hooluh-
hiki-dooluh uddurwise known us duh Royul Umbilicul Bengul
Cakewalk comes frum duh lan were duh goils bade in nachurl
shampain tree times uh day un doan wear nutn between duh
knees un duh neck evrybudy wise up tuh dis fac duh managemunt is incloodin Princess Anankay's soopurspectaclur ac widout extruh charge tuh nobody get dat ladies un gents youse see
her strut her stuff fur duh o-riginul price uv admission no more
no less namely un to wit two bits two five jits five makin fiveun-
twenty ur twentyfive cents duh fort part uv uh silvur dollur all
youse bohs guys bums ginks un nuts wut are treaded fur uh
----- step dis way duh Princess Anankay is about tuh perform
fur duh benefit uv duh Orey-entul EE-lectrickully Lighted
Orphunts' Home un duh boys in genrul uh hiddurto strickly

sacred OO-pee-lah ur Spasmwriggle diereck frum duh temple uv You You walk right up gents duh Princess wears so lidl youse can stick her full uv looks like she wus uh pincushion O dut ticklish dut magnifisunt Huemun Form Divine—. *(Shouts, pointing at* HIM *who stands on the outskirts of the crowd)*—Crawl right up un all fives fellur give duh Princess un fiftyfifty chawnce wid youse kiddo she'll boost yur splendifurous bowlegged blueeyed exterior out uv duh peagreen interior uv pinkpoiple soopurconsciousness fourteen million astrul miles intuh duh prehensile presinks uv predetoimine prehistoric pretarnachurl nutn! *(With a vivid gesture, he pulls aside the curtain. A woman's figure— completely draped in white and holding in its arms a newborn babe at whom it looks fondly—stands, motionless, in the centre of the diminutive room. The crowd recoils.)*

THREE MISS WEIRDS *(Disgustedly, in unison)*: It's all done with mirrors! *(The woman's figure proudly and gradually lifts its head: revealing the face of* ME. HIM *utters a cry of terror. Total darkness—confused ejaculations of rage dwindle swirlingly to entire silence.)*

## Scene VII

SCENE: *The room as it first appeared (Act One, Scene 2), but without* HIM'S *hat on the sofa and with the flowers on the table.* ME *and* HIM *occupy the same positions with respect to each other and to the room itself as when Scene 5 of Act Three was interrupted by darkness.*

ME: I am thinking.

HIM: And may I ask what you are thinking?—Anything everything nothing or something: which is it?

ME: The last.

HIM: Something?

ME: Something.

HIM (*After a pause*): Is it something about the window?

ME: No.

HIM: About the door?

ME: No.

HIM: About what's behind you?

ME: Not exactly. No.

HIM: But you're thinking something about this room, aren't you?

ME: Yes, I'm thinking something about this room.

HIM: I'm afraid that you'll have to tell me what you are thinking.

ME: Can't you guess? I'll give you time.

HIM: Time is the because with which some dolls are stuffed. No, I can't guess.

ME (*Quietly*): It has only three walls.

HIM (*Looks about him in astonishment*): Behind you—that's a wall, isn't it?

ME: That's one.

HIM: One—and what's there? (*Pointing to the door wall*)

ME: A wall.

HIM: Two—and there? (*Pointing over his shoulder to the window wall behind him*)

ME: Three.

HIM: Three—and what do you see there? (*Indicating the invisible wall*)

ME: People.

HIM (*Starts*): What sort of people?

ME: Real people. And do you know what they're doing?

HIM (*Stares at her*): What are they doing?

ME (*Walking slowly upstage toward the door*): They're pretending that this room and you and I are real. (*At the door, turning, faces the audience*)

HIM *(Standing in the middle of the room, whispers)*: I wish I could believe this.

ME *(Smiles, shaking her head)*: You can't.

HIM *(Staring at the invisible wall)*: Why?

ME: Because this is true.

· CURTAIN ·

# ANTHROPOS

## or

# THE FUTURE OF ART

SCENE: *one-half of the dim interior of a hemispherical cave. In the fore-ground—to the audience's left, three uncouth infrahuman crea-tures smothered in filthy skins squat, warming their gnarled paws at what was once a fire—to the audience's right, a naked man (his back toward the trio) is cautiously, with a few crude painting tools, outlining some monster on the upcurving wall before him. In the central background hangs a curtain of skins: somewhere behind this curtain, a sequence of rattling gushing hissing rumbling clanking noises repeats itself without interruption.*

FIRST INFRAHUMAN CREATURE *(staring at the embers, speaks grayly)*: Well, as I was saying . . .
SECOND INFRAHUMAN CREATURE *(ditto)*: Ugh-huh.
THIRD INFRAHUMAN CREATURE *(ditto)*: I know what you mean, G.

*A pause. All three stare dully at the embers. The man continues to paint, warily and precisely, on the wall before him.*

SECOND INFRAHUMAN CREATURE: What we need is a slogan.
FIRST INFRAHUMAN CREATURE: Absolutely.
THIRD INFRAHUMAN CREATURE: That's talking, O, my boy.
FIRST INFRAHUMAN CREATURE: You're on the right track, O.

*Another pause. The three stare. The outline grows.*

THIRD INFRAHUMAN CREATURE: How do you like this?
FIRST INFRAHUMAN CREATURE: Which?
THIRD INFRAHUMAN CREATURE: "Taboogeyman'll get you if you don't watch out."

SECOND INFRAHUMAN CREATURE: Too long, D, too long.

FIRST INFRAHUMAN CREATURE: And much too true.

*Another pause. The three stare. Planes begin.*

SECOND INFRAHUMAN CREATURE: I have an idea.

FIRST INFRAHUMAN CREATURE: No!

THIRD INFRAHUMAN CREATURE: Let's hear it, O.

SECOND INFRAHUMAN CREATURE: "Save your sorrows for tomorrows."

FIRST INFRAHUMAN CREATURE: Pretty weak. *(To 3rd)* What do you say, D?

THIRD INFRAHUMAN CREATURE: Sure. They want something more positive.

*Another pause. The three stare. Tones build.*

FIRST INFRAHUMAN CREATURE: Here's a beaut.

SECOND INFRAHUMAN CREATURE: Ye-ay-uh?

FIRST INFRAHUMAN CREATURE: "Get wise to yourself."

THIRD INFRAHUMAN CREATURE: Nn-nn.

SECOND INFRAHUMAN CREATURE: Too matter-of-fact.

THIRD INFRAHUMAN CREATURE: You must interest their imaginations, G.

SECOND INFRAHUMAN CREATURE: They're just children after all, you know.

*Another pause. The three stare. Masses coalesce.*

THIRD INFRAHUMAN CREATURE: Listen.

FIRST INFRAHUMAN CREATURE: WELL?

THIRD INFRAHUMAN CREATURE: "Time is money."

FIRST INFRAHUMAN CREATURE: Nothing doing.

SECOND INFRAHUMAN CREATURE: We've got to kid 'em along. *(To 1st)* Haven't we, G?

FIRST INFRAHUMAN CREATURE: Remember, D, they have sensibilities.

SECOND INFRAHUMAN CREATURE: Why not appeal to their higher natures, eh?

FIRST INFRAHUMAN CREATURE: That's the stuff, O; give 'em something ideelistic.

*Another pause. The three stare. Volumes poise.*

SECOND INFRAHUMAN CREATURE: I've thought of a peach!

FIRST INFRAHUMAN CREATURE: Fire away, O.

SECOND INFRAHUMAN CREATURE: "It's crucified."

FIRST INFRAHUMAN CREATURE: Rotten.

THIRD INFRAHUMAN CREATURE: No punch.

FIRST INFRAHUMAN CREATURE: Insipid.

THIRD INFRAHUMAN CREATURE: Lacks pep.

FIRST INFRAHUMAN CREATURE: Too psychological.

THIRD INFRAHUMAN CREATURE: They wouldn't understand it.

*Another pause. The three stare. Color weaves.*

FIRST INFRAHUMAN CREATURE: Zowie!

SECOND INFRAHUMAN CREATURE: Shoot, G!

THIRD INFRAHUMAN CREATURE: Spit it out, G, old man!

SECOND INFRAHUMAN CREATURE: Come clean!

THIRD INFRAHUMAN CREATURE: Make it snappy!

SECOND INFRAHUMAN CREATURE: Shake a leg!

THIRD INFRAHUMAN CREATURE: Let's go!

FIRST INFRAHUMAN CREATURE: "Nothing succeeds like success."

SECOND INFRAHUMAN CREATURE: AWFUL.
THIRD INFRAHUMAN CREATURE: I should say NOT.

*Another pause. The three stare. The elephantine design has not quite achieved itself—the man hesitates, perplexed.*

ALL THREE INFRAHUMAN CREATURES *(simultaneously)*: I GOT IT!

*They leap up.*

FIRST INFRAHUMAN CREATURE: "Ev-
SECOND INFRAHUMAN CREATURE: O-
THIRD INFRAHUMAN CREATURE: Lution."
ALL THREE INFRAHUMAN CREATURES: HOORAY!

*They advance toward the footlights, patting each other on the back and shaking hands.*

FIRST INFRAHUMAN CREATURE: Gee—that's SWELL!
SECOND INFRAHUMAN CREATURE: O—BOY!
THIRD INFRAHUMAN CREATURE: DE—CIDEDLY!
FIRST INFRAHUMAN CREATURE: Let's call 'em in: what do you say?
SECOND INFRAHUMAN CREATURE: Sure thing!!
THIRD INFRAHUMAN CREATURE: Posi-tively!

*All three, facing the audience, whistle shrilly through their fingers— whereupon a muttering snarling grunting squeaking jabbering mob of hide-smothered infrahuman dwarfs angrily seethes down the center aisle toward the footlights.*

FIRST INFRAHUMAN CREATURE *(straightening)*: At-
SECOND INFRAHUMAN CREATURE: Ten-

THIRD INFRAHUMAN CREATURE: TION!

*The onrushing mob freezes into a silent mass whose units punctually and simultaneously salute—the salute is languidly returned by the trio.*

FIRST INFRAHUMAN CREATURE: Men—the war will soon be over!
SECOND INFRAHUMAN CREATURE: Evolution is our ally!
THIRD INFRAHUMAN CREATURE: Three cheers for Evolution!
MOB OF INFRAHUMAN DWARFS: RAH—RAH—RAH.
FIRST INFRAHUMAN CREATURE: About—face!

*The mob obeys.*

SECOND INFRAHUMAN CREATURE: Forward—
THIRD INFRAHUMAN CREATURE: March!

*Exit the silent mob, marching up the center aisle in good order.*

FIRST INFRAHUMAN CREATURE *(relaxing)*: Whew!
SECOND INFRAHUMAN CREATURE: Pretty neat, the way they took it—eh?
THIRD INFRAHUMAN CREATURE: I'll say so!

*The naked man, who has neither heard nor seen the preceding action, lays down carefully his painting tools, casts a brief look at his uncompleted work and walks briskly upstage toward the curtain of hides which hangs in the central background.*

FIRST INFRAHUMAN CREATURE *(catching sight of the man for the first time, recoils and shrieks)*: Look!

*He points. The man, surprised, pauses.*

SECOND INFRAHUMAN CREATURE *(looking, screams)*: Help!

THIRD INFRAHUMAN CREATURE *(seeing, starts violently)*: What the hell is that thing doing!

MAN *(shrugging his shoulders)*: I'm stuck.

FIRST INFRAHUMAN CREATURE *(to 2nd and 3rd)*: What does it mean: "Stuck"?

SECOND INFRAHUMAN CREATURE *(to 1st and 3rd)*: How the devil did it get in, anyway?

THIRD INFRAHUMAN CREATURE *(to 1st and 2nd)*: Where does it think it's going?

MAN *(nodding toward the background curtain)*: I've got to have another look.

*He makes for the curtain.*

FIRST INFRAHUMAN CREATURE *(plucking up courage)*: Wait a decade!

*The man pauses.*

SECOND INFRAHUMAN CREATURE: What's the big idea?

THIRD INFRAHUMAN CREATURE: "Another look" at which?

MAN *(nodding toward the background curtain)*: That mammoth.

FIRST INFRAHUMAN CREATURE *(mystified)*: "Mammoth"?

SECOND INFRAHUMAN CREATURE *(horrified)*: What "mammoth"?

THIRD INFRAHUMAN CREATURE *(anguished)*: Where?

MAN *(pointing to the curtain)*: Outside, there.

FIRST INFRAHUMAN CREATURE *(uncomprehendingly)*: "Outside"—?

SECOND INFRAHUMAN CREATURE *(incredulously, to 1st and 3rd)*: Does it mean there are still mammoths?

THIRD INFRAHUMAN CREATURE *(stupefied, to 1st and 2nd)*: Doesn't realize ages have elapsed?

MAN *(arms akimbo, frowns)*: What are you three freaks talking about?

FIRST INFRAHUMAN CREATURE *(ardently)*: Civilization!

SECOND INFRAHUMAN CREATURE *(fervently)*: Emancipation!

THIRD INFRAHUMAN CREATURE *(enthusiastically)*: Progress!

MAN *(grins)*: Don't try to kid me!

FIRST INFRAHUMAN CREATURE *(earnestly)*: No, reely!

SECOND INFRAHUMAN CREATURE *(pompously)*: It's the Ford's truth!

THIRD INFRAHUMAN CREATURE *(solemnly)*: So help me Lenin!

MAN *(still grinning)*: Yes? *(Stepping crisply to the curtain, he seizes it and yanks it aside—revealing a jagged cave-mouth and, beyond, a sunlit excavation wherein a solitary rattling gushing hissing rumbling clanking steamshovel is rotating and plunging and rearing and wheeling and spewing.—The trio of infrahuman creatures, speared by instreaming sunlight, yells: the man, quickly half-turning, lifts one hand in an imperious gesture of warning, and whispers)*: Sh!

FIRST INFRAHUMAN CREATURE *(its teeth chattering with terror)*: What the—

MAN *(scowling, whispers imperiously)*: Don't scare him!

SECOND INFRAHUMAN CREATURE *(quaking)*: "Scare him"—?

THIRD INFRAHUMAN CREATURE *(tottering)*: "Scare"—who?

MAN *(cautiously indicating the steamshovel, whispers)*: That mammoth! *(Confidentially)*: They're very timid! *(Stealthily falls on hands and knees: whispers)*: So long!

*Warily creeps through the cave-mouth, and onward in the direction of the steamshovel: occasionally halting, to flatten himself on the earth.*

FIRST INFRAHUMAN CREATURE *(flabbergasted, to 3rd)*: Ugh-huh.

*Tearing himself from the spear of sunlight, he cringes to the fire; the third follows suit: both squat, quivering, warming their gnarled paws and staring at the embers.*

SECOND INFRAHUMAN CREATURE: I know what you mean.

*Slinking up the sunspear to the very cave-mouth, he violently pulls the curtain—the entire cave darkens: he staggers to the embers, squats, shuddering: stares.*

THIRD INFRAHUMAN CREATURE *(grayly, to itself)*: Well, as I was saying . . .

· CURTAIN ·

# SANTA CLAUS

## A Morality

For Fritz Wittels

# CHARACTERS

Death
Santa Claus
Mob
Child
Woman

## Scene I

SCENE: *(Death, strolling—he wears black tights on which the bones of his skeleton are vividly suggested by daubs of white paint, and his mask imitates crudely the face of a fleshless human skull. Enter, slowly and despondently, a prodigiously paunchy figure in faded red motheaten Santa Claus costume, with the familiar Santa Claus maskface of a bewhiskered jolly old man.)*

DEATH: Something wrong, brother?

SANTA CLAUS:              Yes.

DEATH:                   Sick?

SANTA CLAUS:                    Sick at heart.

DEATH: What seems to be the trouble? Come—speak out.

SANTA CLAUS: I have so much to give; and nobody will take.

DEATH: My problem is also one of distribution, only it happens to be the other way round.

SANTA CLAUS: The other way round?

DEATH:                Quite.

SANTA CLAUS:                  What do you mean?

DEATH:                                                I mean
I have so much to take; and nobody will give.

SANTA CLAUS: Strange.

DEATH:                    Strange, indeed. But this is even stranger:
I'm certain I can help you.

SANTA CLAUS:                    Very kind—

DEATH: Tut, tut; who helps another helps himself
Now if I may be allowed to analyze your case—

SANTA CLAUS: Analyze?

DEATH:            Listen. You're trying to give people something—right?

SANTA CLAUS: Right.

DEATH:                    And people won't take it?

SANTA CLAUS:                                        Right.

DEATH: Why not?

SANTA CLAUS:            Why not, indeed, I wish I knew.

DEATH: Because, my poor misguided friend, they can't.

SANTA CLAUS: Can't?

DEATH:                    Cannot.

SANTA CLAUS:                    But surely nothing could be simpler
than taking something which is freely offered?

DEATH: You're speaking of a true or actual world.
Imagine, if you can, a world so blurred
that its inhabitants are one another
—an idiotic monster of negation:
so timid, it would rather starve itself
eternally than run the risk of choking;
so greedy, nothing satisfies its hunger
but always huger quantities of nothing—
a world so lazy that it cannot dream;
so blind, it worships its own ugliness:
a world so false, so trivial, so unso,

phantoms are solid by comparison.

But no—you can't imagine such a world.

SANTA CLAUS: Any more than such a world could imagine me.

DEATH: Very good. Now as to this ungivable something you're trying to give, this gift which nobody can take—what, just exactly, is it?

SANTA CLAUS:     I don't know.

DEATH: I do.

SANTA CLAUS: Do you?

DEATH:               Yes. It is understanding.

SANTA CLAUS: Understanding?

DEATH:                    Yes.

SANTA CLAUS:                    Tell me, how do you know?

DEATH: You told me, when you answered "I don't know."

And when you said you had something to give, you told me;

for isn't understanding the only gift?

Well, there's precisely your predicament.

We are not living in an age of gifts:

this is an age of salesmanship, my friend;

and you are heavy with the only thing

which simply can't be sold.

SANTA CLAUS:                    May I ask you a question?

DEATH: Go right ahead.

SANTA CLAUS:          What's the easiest thing to sell?

DEATH: Knowledge.

SANTA CLAUS:       Knowledge—without understanding?

DEATH: Correct.

SANTA CLAUS:     No.

DEATH:               Absolutely.

SANTA CLAUS:                    But that's absurd!

DEATH: Absurd—and also tragic; yet a fact.

In this empty un-understanding world
anyone can sell knowledge; everybody wants knowledge,
and there's no price people won't pay to get it.
—Become a Scientist and your fortune's made.

SANTA CLAUS: Scientist—?

DEATH: Or, in plain English, a knowledge-salesman.

SANTA CLAUS: I have no knowledge . . . only understanding—

DEATH: Forget your understanding for a while,
    *(he plucks off Santa Claus' mask, revealing a young man's face)*
and as for knowledge, why, don't let that worry you:
    *(he slips off his own mask, revealing a fleshless human skull,*
    *and crams the skull mask over the young face of Santa Claus)*
once people hear the magic name of "Science"
    *(slipping the Santa Claus mask over his own skull face)*
you can sell people anything—except understanding.

SANTA CLAUS: Yes?

DEATH: Anything at all.

SANTA CLAUS: You mean, provided—

DEATH: Provided nothing!

SANTA CLAUS: You don't mean to tell me
I could sell people something which didn't exist?

DEATH: Why not? You don't suppose people exist, do you?

SANTA CLAUS: Don't people exist?

DEATH: People?—I'll say they don't!
I wish to heaven they did exist; in that case
I shouldn't be the skeleton I am.
No—in this "Science" game, this "knowledge" racket,
infinity's your limit; but remember:
the less something exists, the more people want it.

SANTA CLAUS: I can't seem to think of anything which doesn't exist
—perhaps you could help me.

DEATH: How about a wheelmine?

SANTA CLAUS: A wheelmine?

DEATH: Surely a wheelmine doesn't exist and never will, and never has existed.

SANTA CLAUS: A wheelmine . . . but that's perfectly fantastic!

DEATH: Why say "fantastic" when you mean "Scientific"?

—Well, I'll be strolling. So long, Mister Scientist!

## Scene II

SCENE: *(Santa Claus, masked as Death, haranguing a Mob)*

SANTA CLAUS: Hear ye! Hear ye! Hear ye! I am a Scientist!
And just to prove it, ladies and gentlemen,
I'll tell you anything you want to know.
—Go ahead: ask me something; anything.

VOICE: Mister.

SANTA CLAUS: Yes?

VOICE: How can I make a million dollars?

SANTA CLAUS: A million dollars—is that all you want?

VOICE: Well, I could use a couple, if you've got 'em.

SANTA CLAUS: Could you use ten or twelve?

VOICE: Ten or twelve million dollars?
—O, boy!

SANTA CLAUS: You're kidding.

VOICE: Kidding! Why, you can't tell me anything I wouldn't do for ten or twelve million.

SANTA CLAUS: I'll bet you I can.

VOICE: O yeah? How much'll you bet?

SANTA CLAUS: I'll bet a dollar.

VOICE: You're on! What wouldn't I do?

SANTA CLAUS: You wouldn't spend five hundred measly dollars for a share of preferred stock in a giltedged wheelmine.

VOICE: Wheelmine?

SANTA CLAUS: Don't tell me you never heard of a wheelmine!

VOICE: Well, maybe—

SANTA CLAUS: Maybe you don't even know what wheels are.

VOICE: Wheels?

SANTA CLAUS: They're the things that make the world go round.

VOICE: Sure, I know wheels—why, wheels are everywhere.

SANTA CLAUS: I'll say they are: including people's heads
    —now can you tell me what a mine is?

VOICE:                                    A mine?
    Why, a mine is a hole in the ground.

SANTA CLAUS:                              Now can you tell me what
    one and one make?

VOICE:                 One and one?

SANTA CLAUS:                       Yes.

VOICE:                       Two.

SANTA CLAUS: You're wonderful! My boy, with a brain like that
    you ought to be President of the United States
    —now listen carefully: one and one make two;
    but what do wheel and mine make?

VOICE:                              They make wheelmine.

SANTA CLAUS: Congratulations! You know everything—

VOICE: But people don't dig wheels out of the ground.

SANTA CLAUS: I'll say people don't!

VOICE:                     Well, who does?

SANTA CLAUS:                       Can't you guess?

VOICE: Science?

SANTA CLAUS: By Jove, you're just another Einstein!
    I certainly was a fool to bet with you
    —here's your certificate of preferred stock.

VOICE: Here's your five hundred dollars—

SANTA CLAUS:                     Five hundred? Listen:

you may have been dealing with conmen all your life,
but I'm a Scientist: here's the dollar you won.

VOICE: Thanks, mister.

SANTA CLAUS:          You're quite welcome.—Anybody else?

VOICES: Me! Me, too! Gimme!

SANTA CLAUS:                —Just a moment. Friends,
it never shall be said that Science favored
or slighted anyone. Remember: Science
is no mere individual. Individuals
are, after all, nothing but human beings;
and human beings are corruptible:
for (as you doubtless know) to err is human.
Think—only think! for untold centuries
this earth was overrun by human beings!
Think: it was not so many years ago
that individuals could be found among us!
O those dark ages! What a darkness, friends!
But now that hideous darkness turns to light;
the flame of Science blazes far and wide:
Science, impartial and omnipotent,
before whose superhuman radiance
all dark prescientific instincts vanish.
Think—only think! at last the monster, man,
is freed from his obscene humanity!
—While men were merely men, and nothing more,
what was equality? A word. A dream.
Men never could be equal—why? Because
equality's the attribute of supermen
like you, and you, and you, and you. And therefore
(superladies and supergentlemen)
when the impartial ear of Science hears
your superhuman voices crying "gimme,"

Science responds in Its omnipotence
"let there be enough wheelmine stock for all."
VOICES: Adda baby! Long live Science! Hooray for wheelmines!

## Scene III

SCENE: *(Death, masked as Santa Claus, strolling: angry voices offstage)*

DEATH: I've got him now!
*(Enter Santa Claus, masked as Death, running)*
—Hello there: what's your hurry?
SANTA CLAUS: Help—quick—for mercy's sake—they're after me—
DEATH: After you?
SANTA CLAUS:     After me, yes! They're coming!
DEATH:                               Who's coming?
SANTA CLAUS: Everybody!
DEATH:           Why?
SANTA CLAUS:               It's the accident—
DEATH:                         Accident?
SANTA CLAUS: To the miners in the mine—
DEATH:                       Miners?
SANTA CLAUS:                             Wheelminers!
DEATH: Are you crazy?
SANTA CLAUS:     I don't know—will you tell me something?
DEATH: Tell you what.
SANTA CLAUS:       Does a wheelmine exist, or doesn't it?
DEATH: A wheelmine?
SANTA CLAUS:         Yes.
DEATH:               Don't be ridiculous.
SANTA CLAUS: You mean it doesn't exist?
DEATH:                           Exist? Of course not!
SANTA CLAUS: In other words, a wheelmine is nonexistent isn't it?

DEATH: Perfectly.

SANTA CLAUS:     O, then tell me; tell me:
  how can it maim, how can it mutilate;
  how can it turn mere people into monsters:
  answer me—how!

DEATH:                 My friend, you've forgotten something:
  namely, that people, like wheelmines, don't exist
  —two negatives, you know, make an affirmative.
  Now if I may be allowed to analyze—

SANTA CLAUS:                              Do you want to die?

DEATH: I die? Ha-ha-ha-ha! How could Death die?

SANTA CLAUS: —Death?

DEATH:                 Didn't you know?

SANTA CLAUS:                 I'm going mad. You: tell me,
  whatever you are, Death or the Devil, tell me:
  how can I prove I'm not to blame for the damage
  caused by an accident which never happened
  to people who are nonexistent?

DEATH:                 You can't.

SANTA CLAUS: My God—but what am I going to do, then?

DEATH:                                      Do?
  Why, my dear fellow, it looks to me as if
  you'd have to prove you don't exist yourself.

SANTA CLAUS: But that's absurd!

DEATH:                 —And tragic; yet a fact.
  So make it snappy, Mister Santa Claus!
      *(Exit. From the opposite direction enter Mob, furious: a little
      girl follows)*

VOICES: There he is! Grab him! Listen, Mister Science
  —you're going to hang for this!

SANTA CLAUS:                 What do you mean?

A VOICE: You know what we mean!

149

SANTA CLAUS:                          Why, who do you think I am?

ANOTHER: Think? We don't think; we know! You're Science!

SANTA CLAUS:                                              Science?

ANOTHER: Science—the crook who sold us stock in a wheelmine!

ANOTHER: Science—the beast who buries men alive!

SANTA CLAUS:                                          —Stop!

> Ladies and gentlemen, this is all a mistake:
> I am not Science; wheelmines don't exist,
> and as for burying people alive—that's nonsense.

VOICES: We say you're Science! Down with Science!

SANTA CLAUS:                                          —Wait!

> Ladies and gentlemen: if you all have been
> deceived by some impostor—so have I.
> If you all have been tricked and ruined—so have I.
> And so has every man and woman, I say.
> I say it, and you feel it in your hearts:
> we are all of us no longer glad and whole,
> we have all of us sold our spirits into death,
> we are all of us the sick parts of a sick thing,
> we have all of us lost our living honesty,
> and so we are all of us not any more ourselves.
> —Who can tell truth from falsehood any more?
> I say it, and you feel it in your hearts:
> no man or woman on this big small earth.
> —How should our sages miss the mark of life,
> and our most skillful players lose the game?
> your hearts will tell you, as my heart has told me:
> because all know, and no one understands.
> —O, we are all so very full of knowing
> that we are empty: empty of understanding;
> but, by that emptiness, I swear to you
> (and if I lie, ladies and gentlemen,

hang me a little higher than the sky)
all men and every woman may be wrong;
but nobody who lives can fool a child.
—Now I'll abide by the verdict of that little girl
over there, with the yellow hair and the blue eyes.
I'll simply ask her who I am; and whoever
she says I am, I am: is that fair enough?

VOICES: Okay! Sure! Why not? Fine! A swell idea!
The kid will tell him who he is, all right!
Everybody knows!

SANTA CLAUS:                    —Silence! *(To Child)* Don't be afraid: who
am I?

CHILD:     You are Santa Claus.

VOICES:                         . . . Santa Claus?

CHORUS: Ha-ha-ha-ha—there ain't no Santa Claus!

SANTA CLAUS: Then, ladies and gentlemen, I don't exist.
And since I don't exist, I am not guilty.
And since I am not guilty, I am innocent.
—Goodbye! And, next time, look before you leap.
        *(Exit. Mob disintegrates slowly, muttering.)*


## Scene IV

SCENE: *(Santa Claus, masked as Death, strolling)*


SANTA CLAUS: That was a beautiful child . . . If only I were sure—
        *(Enter Death, masked as Santa Claus)*
Hello there!

DEATH:             O—hello. You're looking better.

SANTA CLAUS: Better? Why not?

DEATH:                         I take it, my advice proved
efficacious?

SANTA CLAUS:     Death, you've saved my life!

DEATH: You don't say so.

SANTA CLAUS:          Absolutely!

DEATH:                    Well, my friend, I'm going to
ask you to do me a favor now.

SANTA CLAUS: Go right ahead!

DEATH:                    I've got a heavy date
with a swell jane up the street a little way,
but something tells me she prefers plump fellows.
Will you give me your fat and take my skeleton?

SANTA CLAUS: With all the pleasure in the world, old-timer; and I'll
throw in a wheelmine, just for luck!

DEATH: No wheelmines, thank you.

     *(They undress)*

SANTA CLAUS:                    That was a beautiful child.

DEATH: —Child?

SANTA CLAUS:     I was . . .

DEATH:                    Thinking of the old days, eh? Well, children are your specialty.

SANTA CLAUS:               I love them.
I have always loved them, and I shall love them always.

     *(They exchange costumes; and dress as each other)*

DEATH: De gustibus non disputandum est;
or, in good American: I prefer women.

SANTA CLAUS: Have you ever loved a woman?

DEATH:                         Pardon me, did you
say "loved"?

SANTA CLAUS:     I said "loved."

DEATH:                    No. Have you?

SANTA CLAUS: Once.

DEATH:           Well, everybody makes mistakes
—I'll see you later. So long, Mister Death!

*(Exit Death as Santa Claus, paunchily swaggering. From the opposite direction enter, on tiptoe, Child)*

CHILD: Hello.

SANTA CLAUS: —Well, hello!

CHILD: You remember me?

SANTA CLAUS: Of course I do.

CHILD: You're different, aren't you.

SANTA CLAUS: Yes; I am.

CHILD: Much thinner.

SANTA CLAUS: Do you like me this way?

CHILD: I guess . . . I like you any way—if you're you.

SANTA CLAUS: I guess that makes me very happy.

CHILD: But I guess . . .

SANTA CLAUS: What do you guess?

CHILD: You could be happier, couldn't you?

SANTA CLAUS: Perhaps I could.

CHILD: —Because you're looking for somebody?

SANTA CLAUS: I am.

CHILD: And I'm looking for somebody, too.

SANTA CLAUS: Somebody very beautiful?

CHILD: O, yes; she's very beautiful. And very sad.

SANTA CLAUS: Very beautiful and very sad. Tell me: is she sad because she lost you?

CHILD: Because we lost each other—and somebody else.

*(Confused voices, far offstage)*

Goodbye—

SANTA CLAUS: Why are you going?

CHILD: Don't be afraid: we'll find her.

SANTA CLAUS:     I should never be afraid
    of anything in the sky and on the earth
    and anywhere and everywhere and nowhere,
    if I were only sure of one thing.
CHILD:                                What.
SANTA CLAUS: Who was that somebody else?
CHILD:                                That somebody we
    lost?
SANTA CLAUS: Yes.
CHILD:              Can't you guess who?
SANTA CLAUS:              Can I?
CHILD:                                You.
        *(She dances away)*


## Scene V

SCENE: *(Enter Woman, weeping)*


WOMAN: Knowledge has taken love out of the world
    and all the world is empty empty empty:
    men are not men any more in all the world
    for a man who cannot love is not a man,
    and only a woman in love can be a woman;
    and, from their love alone, joy is born—joy!
    Knowledge has taken love out of the world
    and all the world is joyless joyless joyless.
    Come, death! for I have lost my joy and I
    have lost my love and I have lost myself.
        *(Enter Santa Claus, as Death)*
    You have wanted me. Now take me.
SANTA CLAUS:                        Now and forever.

WOMAN: How fortunate is dying, since I seem
    to hear his voice again.

VOICE *(offstage)*:           Dead! Dead!

WOMAN: Could the world be emptier?

    *(Tumult offstage. She cringes)*

SANTA CLAUS:           Don't be afraid.

WOMAN: O voice of him I loved more than my life,
    Protect me from that deathless lifelessness—.

    *(Enter Mob in procession, reeling and capering: the last Mob-*
    *sters carry a pole, from which dangles the capering and reeling*
    *corpse of Death disguised as Santa Claus.)*

CHORUS: Dead. Dead. Dead. Dead. Dead.

VOICES: Hooray! Dead; yes, dead: dead. Hooray!
    Science is dead! Dead. Science is dead!

VOICE: He'll never sell another wheelmine—never!

VOICES: Dead! Hooray! Dead! Hooray! Dead!

VOICE: The filthy lousy stinking son of a bitch.

CHORUS: Hooray hooray hooray hooray hooray!

A VOICE: He fooled us once, and once was once too much!

ANOTHER: He never fooled us, pal: it was the kid.

    *(Woman starts)*

ANOTHER: Yeah, but the second time—boy, was that good!

ANOTHER: I'll say it was!

ANOTHER:           Did you see the look she gave him?

ANOTHER: Did you hear her say *"that* isn't Santa Claus"?

    *(Woman turns: sees the dangling effigy—recoils from the real*
    *Santa Claus)*

CHORUS: Ha-ha-ha-ha—there ain't no Santa Claus!

    *(Exit Mob, reeling and capering, booing whistling screeching)*

WOMAN: Yes, the world could be emptier.

SANTA CLAUS:           Now and—

WOMAN:                                                    Never.

    I had remembered love—but who am I?

    Thanks, Death, for making love remember me.

      *(Enter dancing Child: sees Woman, and rushes to her arms)*

WOMAN: Joy—joy! My (yes; O, yes) my life my love

    my soul myself . . . —Not yours, Death!

SANTA CLAUS *(unmasking)*:                    No.

WOMAN *(kneeling to Santa Claus)*:              Ours.


• CURTAIN •

# TOM

A Ballet

To Marion Morehouse who suggested that I make
a ballet based on "Uncle Tom's Cabin"

# Synopsis

At the Kentucky plantation of highly respectable Mr Shelby, the black slaves, led by Tom, are engaged in a revival meeting. Their religious ecstacies are crowned by the appearance of the master and mistress. Mrs Shelby is followed by Eliza, her mulatto maid, who holds her baby in her arms. The Shelbys dance; Tom and the other black slaves applaud.—Meanwhile, unnoticed by whites and blacks, Eliza's mulatto husband, George, enters; exhausted and covered with blood. Eliza, rallying her courage, exhorts him to escape. Inspired by the sight of their child, he makes a break for freedom.— The Shelbys' dance is rudely interrupted when Haley, a slavetrader with whom Shelby has had secret business dealings, arrives. Haley threatens Shelby with a mortgage, which the slavetrader offers to exchange for Tom and Eliza; Mrs Shelby, horrified, begs Haley to take her jewels instead: he refuses. Griefstricken, Mrs Shelby departs. Shelby, furious but helpless, pockets the mortgage and goes; leaving Tom and Eliza at Haley's mercy.—After a triumphant dance, Haley advances to seize his new property; but Eliza flees with her child. Haley immediately summons a band of slavecatchers, who rush out in pursuit of Eliza. Tom makes no attempt to escape.

## EPISODE TWO

From the further bank of a river filled with floating icecakes, Eliza, pursued by Haley's slavecatchers, leaps with her child. Landing on one of the icecakes, she collapses; but, as it tilts, she jumps to another; then to another: and so crosses the river, temporarily thwarting her pursuers.—The scene shifts to a tavern. George arrives, disguised as a Spanish gentleman. Before a multitude of carousers he dances, at first in character; then recklessly: finally he tears off his disguise. At this moment, the carousers are revealed as Haley's slavecatchers.—We return to Eliza: overcome with fatigue, she has fallen with her child clutched in her arms: she seems lost. But a vision of her mother, Cassy, being beaten by a brutal master, Legree, gives Eliza the strength of desperation; and she rises.—George and the slavecatchers find Eliza at the same instant. The slavecatchers, advancing confidently to seize their double prey, are unexpectedly checked by the appearance of groups of Quakers or Friends. Armed only with the Inner Light of personal communion, the Friends of humanity rout its foes.—A new world opens to the fugitives, who thankfully celebrate their escape; consecrating their child to freedom.

## EPISODE THREE

We arrive at the magnificent New Orleans estate of StClare, a young Southern aristocrat. Beautiful Creole slaves are everywhere. The atmosphere combines languor and refinement.—Suddenly an incorrigible little black slave, Topsy, enters; upsetting the household and colliding with StClare's New England cousin, Miss Ophelia (called by the slaves "Miss Feely") who acts as his housekeeper. StClare, entering, rescues Topsy from Miss Feely's wrath by inviting Miss Feely to dance with him: Topsy joins the dance; Miss Feely, relenting, kisses her.—Eva, StClare's sick daughter, is now carried in by slaves.

Her father tries to coax her attention with huge and magnificent dolls, but Eva does not awaken from her trance. Desperate, StClare prays for inspiration.—As if in answer to his prayer, Tom and Haley appear in the distance. Immediately Eva regains consciousness and, seeing Tom, holds out her arms. StClare, amazed and delighted, buys this new toy from Haley. Miraculously, Tom's very presence heals Eva; who rises and dances to him. Tom joins her, dancing his faith in his Creator. StClare ecstatically dances around them both. But the father's joy is shortlived; for angels appear and, making Eva one of themselves, disappear with her. Before she goes, she gives Tom a locket containing a curl of her golden hair.—Heartbroken, StClare dies; his estate disintegrates. Miss Feely adopts Topsy; the rest of the slaves, including Tom, are put up at auction.—The auction turns out to be an ultrafashionable affair. From a gallery, exquisite ladies watch, applauding each purchaser. A palegold girl and a deep-brown mother and child are sold to elegant gentlemen. Then Tom mounts the block. Two elegant gentlemen bid for him; but Legree, the brutal master of Cassy, Eliza's mother, outbids them both. Tom now belongs to Legree.

## EPISODE FOUR

A ghostly glow shrouds the swampy jungle surrounding Legree's Red River plantation. Legree has just collapsed after a drunken orgy: above and behind him, we see cottonpicking slaves and a slave-driver, all reduced to shadow.—Cassy, rising from her paramour's side, dances unutterable despair; suddenly she takes out a knife: as she is about to kill Legree, Tom intervenes. Cassy commands Tom to escape; Tom, steadfastly praying for her soul, refuses. Cassy's murderous resolution falters.—Legree awakens: his rage, passing from Cassy, falls on Tom. Frenziedly Legree tears in pieces Tom's bible; then, to complete the humiliation of his rescuer, Legree orders Tom to flog Cassy. Tom, refusing, rises to meet his death: Cassy disappears.—When we next see Tom, he is lying alone, almost dead and partially crazed, after a fatal beating by Legree. In his delirium the sufferer tries to strangle himself; and touches Eva's locket. Recovering a little, he takes it from his neck and opens it. When he sees the curl of golden hair, his spirit becomes one with Eva's.—Legree enters. Unaware that the actual Tom is far beyond his reach and that merely the mortal effigy remains, Legree, now absolutely Satanic, resumes the flogging of what he supposes to be his victim. At the moment of Tom's physical death, murderous perversity is confronted by its opposite, Creative Nature: the white killer cringes before an apparition, symbolizing to his distorted senses the vengeance of the entire black race. As this apparition dissolves in the reality of Cassy, Legree's mentality crumbles; the former prodigy of brute strength becomes a miserable insect, consumed by the merciful radiance of eternal things.—Cassy kneels at Tom's feet. Eliza with her child triumphantly enters, followed by George. The raptures of liberation are stilled as wife and husband fall humbly beside Tom. In the midst of this new sorrow, Eliza recognizes her mother, who sees but does not know her. Then the sight of Eliza's child reminds Cassy of Eliza as a little girl; and, beholding her own daughter in the mother of this child, Cassy embraces both Eliza and George.—Suddenly transcending their personalities, the ecstacy of the three brown protagonists overflows. To Judgement trumpets Death enters, black like Tom; and, like Tom's body, Death Itself disappears: appears the Heavenly Host.

# EPISODE ONE

halflight

the stage is a soft grey cube
> centre: a praying pyramidal silence—motionlessly in a circle
> black men and women and children kneel with arms lifted
> toward one black motionlessly erect man

dance of Religious Ecstacy . . . blacks
> the kneeling bodies begin together swaying, their asking arms
> meanwhile fall floatingly and rise; together the praying chil-
> dren women men prostrate slowly and slowly raise themselves;
> together they unkneel, together stand: yearningly around the
> always erect man they whirl writhing upspiral and at his feet
> collapse together.

dance of The Book . . . Tom
> the man stirs. Dilating, he raises in his right hand a book(*);
> he points to the book solemnly with his left hand. Contract-
> ing, he opens cautiously the book: and recoils with wonder.
> Turning the opened bible pages-outward, he slowly traverses
> a ring of corpses—each, resurrected, yearns toward the book;
> kneeling, ecstatically sways: grovelling, wallows. Tightening,
> he kisses the book sacredly. Relaxing, he closes all holiness and
> lays against his heart all wisdom
> > —opening, the wreath of yearnwallowing blacks gradually
> > blossoms across midstage—

before this writhing line of worshippers lovingly Tom
dances to the book, cradling the book as if the book were
a babe; then, lifting his babebook high, falls on both
knees, facing the audience

—light—

enter, middle-backstage, a lady and gentleman emanating trite
intricacies of conventional ballet. Elaborately to stagecentre
the Shelbys advance, followed by a slowly and simply whirling
mulatto girl (Eliza) who holds before her a brown doll. Meanwhile, all the yearngrovelling frantically fallrising blacks, led
by ecstatically twiststraightening Tom, squirmspurt whirlsurg-
ingly outward and at the footlights high together leaping stand;
suddenly
—as the Shelbys, and behind them Eliza, halt.
    Turning, Tom and the blacks hinge, lowbowing to the gra-
ciously gesturing Shelbys; unhinge. Sacredly Tom pockets his
bible. Tom and the blacks march proudly rightward. Lining
the right-front edge of the stage, they stand, facing the Shelbys

dance of The Benevolent Master And Mistress . . . Mr and Mrs
Shelby
    pompously Shelby invites his wife to dance, coyly she accepts:
advancing, they constipate the frontstage with platitudes of
terpsichore. Heartily the blacks, led by clapping Tom, prance a
stampwriggling accompaniment—

enter furtively, left-backstage, a bloodily halfnaked mulatto man
(George). Writheswoonfully dancing in greatening swoops of agony
to Eliza, centre, he collapses at her feet: she boundtwists upward;
fallkneeling, kisses his wounds. He lifts himself a little. She holds

out to him the doll. His woundedness, recognizing its child, rises beside her rising strength. Trembling, she points upward: crumbling, he kisses her, kisses the doll; crumbled, spins clockwise with increasing velocity upstage, becoming taller and taller: while more and more above herself lifting the doll she pivots counterclockwise, more and more slowly sinking into the earth, and—as he disappears right-backstage—crumples; child held high

crouchingly enter a slavetrader (Haley), right-frontstage
   —the blacks rush inward. Tom leaps to Eliza; whose body, swallowing its doll, writhekneels. The dance collapses, left-frontstage; as
      Haley moves by alternate spiderlike outdartings and compressions toward the Shelbys.
      Arriving, he crouchingly salutes mistress and master—
Shelby, drawing himself up, nods stiffly; Mrs Shelby haughtily turns her back. Dartingly Haley indicates Eliza, Tom
      —quiveringly the blacks together cringe. Eliza sinks
      toward Tom; who, kneeling, supports her—
Shelby, producing with exaggerated casualness a huge cigar, shakes his head. Spiderlike, Haley crouches into himself; draws very gradually from his breastpocket and suddenly presents an imposing legal document
      —the blacks freeze—
Shelby starts, drops his cigar, tries to snatch the paper. Haley, recoiling, indicates the contents of the entire stage: bloating, taps the document; leers
      —quiveringly forthcreeping slowly the blacks silently
      secretly approach—
Shelby stamps with futile rage. Mrs Shelby turns inquiringly to her husband, who desperately points at the paper and shrugs helplessly—she recoils: stares, horrified, at

him, at Haley; halfturning, glimpses Eliza, Tom; then, quickly stripping off her bracelets and rings, offers them to Haley
    —lifting all their arms the blacks kneel—
crouchingly Haley declines: dartingly indicates Eliza, Tom
    —praying bodies writhe—
Mrs Shelby's arms drop limply; she bows her head
    —the blacks prostrate themselves. Eliza, suddenly straightening, clutches her doll. Tom, sacredly taking from his pocket the book, holds it over his heart
exit slowly, left-frontstage, Mrs Shelby; burying her face against Eliza's mute goldenness, against Tom's black silence. As his wife disappears, Shelby nods to Haley: dartingly who hands Shelby the paper—

halflight

—greedily Shelby pockets the mortgage: straightening, shakes both fists at Haley; halfturning toward Eliza and Tom, bows his head guiltily; stooping, goes, left-frontstage dance of the slave-trader . . . Haley
accompanied by rhythmic shuddering swirlings of upwhirling wildly together blacks, Haley embroiders the frontstage with crouchful gloatings, with darting threats, with bloated strut-tings, all focussing on Shelby's cigar—savagely upsnatching which, he slaps it into his mouth; crouched, faces Tom and Eliza
    —whom outsurging suddenly the blacks surround:
Haley takes one step toward them
        —whirlswirling the blacks disintegrate; swirlwhirling disappear, left-backstage.

Haley takes a second step—
 Eliza with her doll twistbounds upward: clock-
 wise whirlingly vanishes, right-backstage; while
 Haley recoils to the footlights. Beckons

—almostdarkness—

everywhere appear luminous dogfaces

dance of The Human Bloodhounds . . . Haley's slavecatchers
 everywhere seethes the almostdarkness with the stalkings
 with the findings with the pouncings of luminously hither-
 and-thither spurting infrahuman figures, orchestrated from
 middle-frontstage by crouchdarting Haley's glowing enor-
 mously cigar—ominously which poises—points, thrice,
 upstage-right
  and seething dogmen disappear

at stagecentre, a kneeling man kisses a book; sacredly tucks it in
a pocket of his ragged trousers: rising,
 slowly advances toward the footlights.
 Pausing, erect, this man extends slowly both arms—
  Haley snakes out handcuffs; snaps them on black wrists
 —Tom(*), uplooking, lifts very gradually his manacled hands:
scooping all the world into all the sky

• BLACKOUT •

# EPISODE TWO

the entire stagefloor is a drifting continuously pattern of irregular squirming brightnesses: elsewhere lives black silence filled with perpetual falling of invisible snow

—spiralling out of high distant darkness, Eliza, with her doll clutched close, drops upon an inmost brightness

dance of Crossing The Icechoked River . . . Eliza
rising: totteringly balancing herself: on the squirming brightness, Eliza leapwhirls to another on which: staggering: she sinks; rises: balancingly: and whirlleaps to another—zigzagging gradually her way outward, toward the audience, from brightness to brightness
hither-and-thither meanwhile, in the high distant darkness from which Eliza came, spurt brutally luminous dogfaces; framing with intricate frustrations her crude whirlleaping-reelsinking-staggerrising-leapwhirling progress.
Precisely when, having almost gained the footlights, Eliza whirlleaps toward an outmost brightness—
the suddenly into itself shriveling lightriver becomes a mere twinkling thread across midstage; and
down out of dark distant height surging together bound dogmen
—between outpouring whom and her a curtain falls: halving the stage

light

Eliza has disappeared

the curtain satirizes a tavern interior; to lower left and right are painted groups of ferociously lolling lifesize carousers, facing the audience, with arms upraised and right hands clutching huge glasses. These drunkards have no faces

—vanitously enter, right-frontstage, a paragon of male elegance

dance of The Snob . . . George disguised
    perfectly, at first, a vitality reduced to egotism imitates itself; artfully posturing, edits all categories of ostentation; generates, depthlessly gesturing, every species of insolent superciliousness. Gradually the linear meaning lessens, the danceplanes express themselves thickly; the puppet becomes a protagonist, the statue assumes manhood. Finally a man rips off a disguise—standing, bloody back to the audience, challenges two groups of painted spectators
        —suddenly who wear the dogmasks of Haley's slave-catchers—

darkness

glowingly dogfaces vanish as the curtain rises on

Eliza(*), prostrate, her doll clutched to her heart:
    in the high distant darkness behind and above Eliza, where luminous dogfaces spurted hither-and-thither, two light-drenched figures appear. One, a mulatto woman (Cassy) resembling Eliza but taller and older, is leaning far backward

with emaciated arms protectingly raised; the other, a huge brutal white man (Legree), is towering over the woman with his right arm lifted and a black whip glittering in his right fist—

slowly Cassy's backwardleaning body outwrithes, yearning toward her daughter

—stumblingly Eliza rises; totterwhirlingly faces the apparition

lightninglike, Legree's whip-fist-arm strikes:

and the vision disappears

—halflight—

George, right-frontstage, whirlleaps inward, catching Eliza when she is about to fall—files of dogmen swoop from left- and right-midstage convergingly outward—enter, right- and left-backstage, a group of men and a group of women (the Friends or Quakers) all dressed in grey; all holding bibles over their hearts

outward swooping files of dogmen meet at the middle foreground—crisply advancing grey figures form a single line across the background in front of George and Eliza

inward surges a single file of dogmen—every Friend lowers his or her bible: and all the Quaker hearts glow with an unearthly radiance

—stopped, the column of attackers flattens itself from within outward; darkening, one after one, the dogmasks sink

back, back a wilted terror cringes—step by crisp step a luminous phalanx marches toward the footlights

—wildly to right and left fleeing Haley's slavecatchers disappear.

The inner wall of the stagecube opens, revealing a peaceful landscape of sunlit mountains

dance of Thankfulness For Freedom . . . the Quakers, George and Eliza
    covering their glowing hearts with their bibles, bowed Friends kneel: George, clasping Eliza, kneels also. Rising, the Friends turn crisply; march erectly toward Eliza and George: rising and lifting slowly Eliza, George leapwhirls outward; halting, back to the audience, at stage-centre. Crisply around high her and erect him surging, the grey phalanx becomes a cross
      certainly a grey cross revolves:
    slowly the luminous Friends raise their bibles;
        proudly George lifts Eliza higher, highest
            slowly proudly Eliza lifts a child toward the mountains

· BLACKOUT ·

# EPISODE THREE

almostlight

right and left, lines of elaborate white columns recedingly
approach each other; between and behind the two inmost columns, at a height corresponding with the appearance of the frus-
trated slavecatchers and with the apparition of Cassy and Legree,
a white parapet is visible: behind this parapet looms lush jungle
foliage. Languorously, at the bases of the columns, lie golden creole girls and boys
     —all of whom upstarting wildly scatter: as

upbounding between inmost columns a totally black dolllike
phenomenon (Topsy) somersaults outward

dance of Instinct Unsubdued . . . Topsy
     highspurting she spreads herself: dropping, contracts: rebound-
          ing, expands—
     squandering unmitigated vitality she handsprings and cart-
          wheels crazily among the fleeing creoles—
     runjumping, she seizes a horizontally jutting element of one
          elaborate capital and swings fiercely to and fro—
     catapulting down, she flings herself on her back and kicks
          madly with wideflung legs—
     upflopping, her wriggling blackness furiously dives in and out
          of the white columns; now pursuing, now pursued by, the
          golden girls and boys

rigidly enter, deepstage, a very angular spinster (Miss Feely)—
colliding with chaos, her mindface registers horror: both her
latharms jerk upward in brittle amazement—she totters; then,
with angry abrupt spasmlike epitomes of movement, advances
the creoles, rushing to the columns, frantically around and
around them circle; as
mightily upplunging in a final convulsion of spontaneity,
Topsy falls flat on her face before the living symbol of disci-
pline—who, tripping over incorrigibility, sprawls headlong
and collapses; motionless, mindface upward

—light—

dwindling the golden circlings fuse in a fluent forthswirling of
boys and girls: enter the elegant essence of Southern aristocracy
(StClare) sniffing a rose
joyously around whom swarms the golden crowd: he lightly
tosses his rose over their heads—the girls rush for it; one,
jumping higher than the rest, snatches it from the air and
sprints offstage, pursued by the other girls and all the boys

magnificently advancing, StClare splendidly pauses before
immobile Topsy and Miss Feely
—Topsy, upbounding, rushes around and around his trousers—Miss Feely, suddenly sitting up, points a dreadful finger at Topsy. Dashing to the nearest pillar, Topsy swarms to
its capital—rising with a lurch, Miss Feely totters Topsyward:
halting, as
StClare, bowing, sumptuously requests the honour of a
dance. Her angularities weaken: courtesying, the spinster
acquiesces

dance of New England And New Orleans . . . Miss Feely and StClare

with all awkwardness illuminating one gracefulness, all prudery underlining one sophistication, decorum and distinction heterogeneously whirl; her purposive vigour conscientiously mangling a mode which his supple sensitivity delicately caricatures

fascinated meanwhile Topsy clings—suddenly sliding earthward, hurls herself between the dancers; oozing such fantastic mimicries that Miss Feely, completely overcome, seizes up the wriggling phenomenon and gives it a hearty kiss

very luxuriously StClare, his task of reconciliation accomplished, turns; bounds gloriously inward to stagecentre; pausing sublimely, beckons—

halflight

between the inmost pair of columns, highlifted by sacredly advancing boyslaves, appears a goldenhaired child(*)

advancing, the creole boys reach stagecentre; pausing, they lower sacredly their golden burden—

sacredly their master, kneeling on one knee, takes from them his daughter (Eva) whose head sinks on her father's shoulder

—dividing, the bowed slaves move slowly rightward and leftward; disappearing right- and left-midstage.

Topsy, suddenly subdued, tiptoes demurely inward beside primly tiptoeing Miss Feely: the pair softly kneel on either side of StClare;

to them, without lifting her head or opening asleep

eyes, Eva dreamily gives pale hands which, bowing, the adorers kiss.

StClare beckons—

from the background tiptoeingly one behind another whirl slowly softly enter the creole girls: each carries sacredly a doll; each doll is larger, more definitely masculine, whiter, and more irrevocably magnificent, than its predecessor. One by one approaching the kneeling father and his sick child, the girls offer the dolls to Eva
whose dreaming head does not move; whose sleeping eyes may not see
one by slowly whirling one the girls, bowed, tiptoe away; disappearing alternately right- and left-midstage
—only when the last girl presents a lifesize doll, resembling in features and dress her father, do Eva's eyes halfopen. For a moment she seems undecided; then her eyelids droop, she slightly shakes her head: and the last girl softly goes—
brokenly StClare bows. After a long instant, he looks upward

enter, at the right extremity of the suddenly shining parapet, Tom; handcuffed; moving with the motionless moving of despair: behind him Haley struts bloatedly
—Eva stirs. Slowly awakening, her opening dolllike eyes passionately search the stage—slowly her golden doll's head turns. Rapturously StClare and Miss Feely and Topsy follow the flowering gaze
—starting, Eva sees Tom. Tom drops on both knees. Haley crouchdarts at Tom: seeing StClare, bows respectfully
—trembling, upyearning, Eva lifts her frail arms toward Tom; slowly, intensely, Tom lifts toward her his manacled hands

quickly StClare signs to Haley, who bows and removes
Tom's handcuffs
   —Eva intensely, slowly, beckons—
      Topsy and Miss Feely upsurge admiringly as,
      quartering the distance from the parapet to Eva
      with one huge ecstatic leap, Tom hurtles out-
      ward between white columns; alighting on both
      knees, both arms joyously wideflung—
         StClare signs to Haley; the slavetrader, low-
         bowingly saluting, disappears

Tom prostrates entirely himself: Miss Feely and Topsy, recoiling,
cling bewilderedly to each other—
   from her father's arms lightly gliding Eva inward moves
      —upstarting, incomparable magnificence leaps back-
      ward—

dance of Heavenly Longing . . . Eva
   to and fro before Tom's bowed self moving with a dolllike
   exactness, she gradually becomes a living child; into this child
   enters something more than life—a new incognizable freedom: which the upward gazing everywhere luminously floating spirit welcomes with fluttering passionately arms
      StClare, meanwhile, circling splendidly around this mirac-
      ulous being, vainly attempts to imitate the mysteries of a not
      imaginable resurrection

dance of Revelation Through The Eternal Word . . . Tom
   upspouting, seizing from his pocket the book, Tom spirals
   heavenward: proudly alights, head thrown back, book held
   high: rushing toward infloating Eva he fallkneels, kisses the

book: upgushing, soars through manycoloured air with high-
waving arms: drops, bowed, book held at arms' length: hurtling toward outswimming Eva he plunges; wallowing, kisses
the book; writhekneels: squirmstands—everywhere then
ecstatically twiststraighteningly spins, vividly pushing the
book upward and hauling vividly it downward; inviting with
immense quickly gestures the heavens to descend: plucking all
the sky into all the world—

notquitedarkness

—together StClare at left- and Tom at right-midstage swoop to
their knees; while floatswimmingly at centrestage descending
Eva hovers—

from between the first and second columns to left-frontstage
and to right-frontstage creep beams of soft radiance: in each
creeping beam quivers a group of childangels. Pirouettingly
the groups, each led by a spirit hovering on shining wings
who holds before her a single shining wing, advance toward
oneanother. Touching, the beams fuse, the angelleaders meet.
Silently the single radiance, gathering itself, goes inward as,
inturning, the leaders float toward Eva: followed by pirouet-
ting pair after pair of quivering spirits

—from whose approach Miss Feely recoils to aghast
StClare; but enraptured Topsy tiptoes toward the inward
moving company.

Arriving at stagecentre, the leaders pause on either side
of Eva; the pairs, dividing, form a fluttering arc behind
her: each leader places a shining wing on Eva's shoulder—meanwhile, all around the angels Topsy ecstatically tiptoes.

Eva, herself an angel, kneels; and, taking from her breast a golden glittering locket, opens it. From behind Eva comes one of the childangels, holding glittering golden shears; the angel cuts a golden curl of Eva's glittering hair and gives the curl to Eva; as the angel resumes her place, Eva lays the golden curl in the glittering locket. Closing the locket, Eva rises and ethereally floating rightward approaches Tom—who, kneeling, with bowed head, his praying arms outstretched, his left hand open, his right hand clutching the book, darkly does not move—lightly she places in his left palm the locket. He does not move. Turning, she swims ethereally leftward toward StClare and Miss Feely—cringing, they hide their faces: stooping, she kisses her father's hair, touches Miss Feely affectionately. Straightening, Eva tiptoes outward to slowly tiptoeing Topsy—both kneel, Eva embraces Topsy, rises: Topsy, on both knees, lifts praying arms toward Eva, who waves a last farewell as eagerly she nears the fluttering expectant angels

    —angular Miss Feely decreases, elegant StClare dwindles—

now highleaping Eva leads all the whirling childangels inward toward the glittering parapet

darkness. A blinding flash of light—

in which Eva and angels disappear, and against which upbounds Topsy with wideflung arms

—halflight

elaborately to right and to left waver the pale columns: wildly
between dizzying them outsurge the golden boys and girls—
     splendid StClare rises, clutching his sumptuous heart
everywhere wilted narrowing spaces reel
          —the father falls.

          Frantically around and around their master's body seethe
          terrified slaves: Miss Feely, diving into the golden swirl,
          drops beside StClare and seizes his hands—recoiling,
          abruptly rising, lurches to Topsy: snatching up black limp-
          ness, totters offstage

Tom(*) stirs
     very gradually his open hand closes on Eva's locket—he
     quivers;
          lifting sacredly the locket, he passes the chain over his head;
          and
               collecting—slowly—himself into himself surges, hugely
               upward:

darkness.

Silence:

     low, clear, and sweet, begins a negro spiritual
          climbingly which wanders (groping) openingly radiates
          hope faith, love
               (hushing the song rebuilds)
          luminously (searching brightly) seeking (gloriously find-
          ing peace, trust, joy)
               deeply (again softly
               enters) whispering grows (mounting
               purely) sweetly (passionately ascending

firmly) marching (seriously) toward a truly (toward a
shining alive) only toward some unimagined Self—

stopped suddenly voices do not sing

—light

the columns and their inhabitants have disappeared, the stage is
a hard grey cube
 centre: a black pyramid—three flights of six stairs, left, middle,
right, converge in a common seventh stair. Passively, between
this triple stairway and the footlights, are standing slaves: old
and young, feeble and strong, men and women and children;
ranging in colour from palegold to jetblack—around and
delicately around whom are strolling ultrafashionable dolllike
gentlemen, gesturing and chatting, pausing occasionally to try
a black biceps or a gold bosom
  the parapet has become a balcony whirlingly aflutter with
dolllike supersophisticated ladies.

enter, at the right extremity of the balcony, an auctioneer. Bowing
effusively, he salutes the dollladies; together who, chatting and
gesturing, face the audience as he moves toward his station, left:
meanwhile, on the stage, dollgentlemen collect to right and to left
of the triplestaircase

dance of The Rival Bidders . . . auctioneer, gentlemen, slaves
 the auctioneer lightly and rapidly hammers, as
  a palegold girl mounts the central flight; revolves gradually like a mannequin on the seventh (top, common) stair:
stands, back to the audience, facing the balcony

the auctioneer pounds heavily once
>a gentleman stands on the first stair of the left flight

the auctioneer pounds twice
>a second gentleman mounts two stairs, right; pauses

the auctioneer pounds thrice
>the first gentleman advances two stairs, pausing on the third (left)

the auctioneer pounds four times
>the second gentleman advances two stairs, pausing on the fourth (right)

the auctioneer pounds five times
>the first gentleman advances two stairs, pausing on the fifth (left)

the auctioneer pounds six times
>the second gentleman advances two stairs, pausing on the sixth (right)

the auctioneer pounds seven times
>neither gentleman moves

solemnly and slowly the auctioneer pounds seven times
>the first gentleman puts a foot on the sixth stair (left); then withdraws his foot

once again the auctioneer pounds seven times, very slowly and very solemnly
>the first gentleman bounds to the seventh (top, common) stair

trivially all the ladies applaud. Thunderously the auctioneer thumps once. Triumphantly the first dollgentleman descends the central flight, followed by his human purchase; parading across the foreground, master and slave disappear—meanwhile, the defeated second dollgentleman strolls down the left side of the pyramid and mingles with his fellows a deepbrown mother and child cringe together up the central stairs; again the dance occurs: mother and child descending disappear with their applauded purchaser

Tom, naked to the waist, slowly and erectly mounts the auctionblock: nudging each other, the dollladies whisper admiringly; while the auctioneer hammers more lightly and rapidly than usual: the dance proceeds, until the auctioneer has twice pounded solemnly and slowly seven times—

halflight.

Enter, right-frontstage, Legree; in a bloodred flare of Satanic radiance:
    with black whip lifted high he immensely bounds among recoiling gentlemen and cowering slaves; then hurtles up the central staircase—
        Tom, spinning with lifted arms, kneels, facing the audience
          —over him towers Legree; bloodily luminous
swoomingly the horrified ladies swirl

· BLACKOUT ·

# EPISODE FOUR

a phosphorescent blur drowns stagecube

dance of The Compelled . . . shadows
    high in this blur stand four unrealities. Three are a man-
like a womanlike a childlike darkness; together these three
silhouettes are leaning far forward, from these three profiles
outspurting shadowhands twitter seizingly and inrush to
again outspurt: on the right of the childlike darkness bloats-
and-dwindles rhythmically a brutish fourth silhouette; its
expanding-and-forshortening shadowarm, continued by a
shadowwhip, emittingly withdraws black lightning—rhythmically as the forwardleaning profiles with outspurtinrushing-
twittering-seizingly hands cringe

lower and nearer, a sprawled thickly drunkenness lies; beside it
a whip

dance of Despair . . . Cassy
    from Legree's tangled bulk cautiously one narrowing spectre
unsheathes itself; beyond this rising apparition climb its ghast-
lier arms: taller by their prayerless leanness a starved height-
ful puppet hoveringly outmoves—utterly slumps suddenly.
Itself gradually lifting, unfurling hopelessly, an emaciation
humanly inhuman drifts; glued to phosphorescent silence,
aimlessly a lost unsubstance roams—spillingly which wilts.
Possibly a less and less being, impossibly a more and more

aspect, livedieingly encircles nearness: dielivingly receding, haunts one sprawled and brutish sameness. Samefully furling, a grey ghost prostrates itself before Legree—over him rising wickedly looms a submarine unreality, awfully delivered of bright widthlessness; crazily his keen doom cradling: his death lifting lovingly

    —as Cassy hangs above him, knife in hand, Legree drunkenly stirs: suddenly the three shadows, upflinging shadowarms, face outward; and the shadowslavedriver pauses, shadowwhip lifted—

Tom, rocketing into stageblur, collapses before Cassy: writhekneeling, hoists at her passionately his bible—

    Cassy's left hand points; softly first to Tom, violently then offstage

—fiercely upshoving the book, Tom shakes his head fiercely

    Cassy's ghostknife wavers

light

with which a stagecube's deepness becomes lush jungle and in which all four shadows dissolve

Legree, whip clutched, surges to his feet; tottering regards Cassy

    Cassy, dropping her knife, leans far backward, both arms protectingly raised

over her he towers; right arm lifted, black whip clenched in right fist. Both are standing as they appeared to Eliza in EPISODE TWO—

    slowly Cassy's backwardleaning body outwrithes, yearning toward the book

—Legree starts: his right fist spits a whip; lunging, he snatches

Tom's bible: seethingly he poises; back to the audience, book held
high
   Cassy drops flat, face downward; as
upspiralling unbelievably Legree tears the book in two—

dance of The Unbook . . . Legree
   out of height thickly swooping, a halfbook in each fist, the
   brute pours greedily into himself—reelboundingly outheav-
   ing, hurls one halfbook away: divecrashing, frenziedly tears a
   fistful of pages from the other—lazily highplunging, vomits
   torn pages into space
      rhythmically meanwhile Tom's kneeling body gutters from
      its anguished hips
   twistfalling crisply through air filled with the book's falltwist-
   ing leaves, brutality upscoops torture: outsurging, shoves suddenly the black whipbutt at black Tom's praying hands: points
   savagely to Cassy
      Tom's head turns; his eyes go from torture to despair—rising,
      stiffening, he hugely raises his both arms and brings black
      them down proudly both with fists clenched to his sides:
      swimmingly erect, floatingly dilated, a man faces Legree
         whose with malice gloating grossness bloats; mightily
         into nervous air whose fist lifts death
            —Cassy's sprouted life glides leftward, disappearing
while between protagonists and audience billowingly lives a
snowy silence screaming crimsonly KILL
      —quickly the red word, the white curtain gradually, die in

almostdarkness.

Stagecentre: a bloody blackness writhing
   glowingly, behind and above writhing, a jungle thrillstirs: not

quite visibly this inhabited background utters glimpsed some-
things, throbs with halfguessed more than known inventions,
hintingly projects not discoverable mysteries of human pain
wallowing Tom pounds madly his breast; bangs, brokenly
upheaving, his skull against the earth, grabs—highrearing his
throat: freezes: drooping; as hands feel goldenness. Crouched
on mashed knees, he passes quiveringly a glittering chain over
his head. Fumbling, with torn fingers opens a shining thing.
Sacredly lifts one glittering wisp

whereupon the jungle background climbingly reveals blue
distance
     out of which tiptoes Eva—an angel—with fluttering faintly
     softly shining wings

dance of The Celestial Certitude . . . Eva(*)
     radiantly her smallness describes intense and more intense cir-
     cles around kneeling bigly him, around a woundedly swoon-
     ing clumsiness which yearns toward the allhealing newly
     mysterious nearness; around a wondering silent deeply more
     than creature: effortlessly whose—nearer becoming nearest—
     skillfulness and magically rises

dance of The Eternal Peace . . . Tom (*)
     weightlessly uplifted within textures beneath knowledge, an
     immortal essence swims; floats a serenity completed, spiritual,
     homogeneous, only composing the most giving freedom of all
     joys which are beyond experience

—gradually inheriting blue distance, Tom and Eva disappear:
     suddenly over blue distance falls a Christian Hell;
          darkly through reddening air a lifesize doll, perfectly

resembling beaten Tom, sinks; flattening limply itself at stagecentre where beaten Tom lay.

Into Hellplanted almostdarkness squirmbounds, clothed with red steadily growing flame, a demon
　　—the Tomdoll spurts up off earth: luxuriously swings before him through Hellspace: at it he leaps—

dance of To Kill . . . Legree
　　not furiously merely but exudingly, not hatefully simply but excretingly, shoots his itlike passion at and with blackly lightning wraps its helike stung prey—flopswooping which spouttumbles. Withfully atishly weaving, a clenched thingbeast sends against a limp manthing ripplesprinting squirmsquirts of darkness. Hellspace swallows jumps, digests flights, spews coastings, of the marvelously everywhere wandering effigy. Hurtling, spurting, a supreme outdivingly entirely inplunging red fiend flogs a mad shadow. Gradually air, annexing earth, marries the slaying and the slain; now two morsels of one nothing caperingly embrace, now through one's poor honest antics flash the other's crisp richly electric gestures
　　—and against Hell anachronistically looming

enters, deepstage, a prodigy of horror: dressed in greencoolish over and under and around herself busily creeping radiance—the goddessmonster of all Africa

dance of Avenging Africa . . . the monstergoddess
　　implacably gliderushing, occultly growpausing, striking like a serpent, dreaming like a forest, one heavenlessly unearthful absence, one kinetically static presence, meaningfully emanates distinct reptilian timelessness, meaninglessly smothers

smoking Hell with the illimitable lushness of impossibility—
suddenly blossoming miraculous abstractions, a doomful
moultingly vast absolute omnipotence points
    the Tomdoll falls
and Nature confronts Satan
    —who tightens, cringing in diminishing fire—

eerily while dilating, fatally perfectly expanding,
    the goddess magically, the monster effortlessly
        opens
            revealing Cassy.

Through himself passing, lightless suddenly Legree emerges in
unselfness

—at unselfness leaps the coolgreen flame of the monstergoddess—

Cassy—uttering ghostly arms—greets

darkness

dance of The Unman . . . Legree masked
    in upgreen and cooldown traveling radiance caught, crouches
    a twittering notness plucked by invisible everywheres of
    anguish; through immaculate devouring lifefulness outpeers,
    transfixed by nowhereish forevers, a dimensionless unbeing
        high at coolgreen who soardarts—inwincing, drops twist-
    edly. Scorched: whirlflops; feetfirst upcurling, spins on
    whose skull: hinging, collapses on whose back—maimed
    squirms. Fro and to, flutterishly, gutters; contracting grov-

els circlingly: outreellifting wholly, springs—into one down
entirely whirlsmiting brightness
    killed, flickers. A quivering smallness; thickeningly
which, in green's lessening cool least, spins; in dim, slow-
lying: in dimmest; slowlier. Slowliest

almostlight

to right and to left whitely rise the sidewalls of a stagecube whose
inner wall equals black curtains
    Legree has vanished: there is no trace of Cassy's disguise.
Cassy herself kneels, back to the audience, at the feet of a real
Tom; whose broken silent blackness sprawls exactly where the
Tomdoll fell

—quickly and simply whirling Eliza with her doll proudly lifted
enters, right-frontstage: behind her, George pours into height;
soaring, descends—
    while leapwhirling freely and joyfully whirlleaping she zig-
    zags ecstatically inward, he handsprings straight across the
    foreground to left-frontstage
        —growingly, at Tom's head, Eliza spirals fast faster: George
        hightwistboundingly inrushes;
            catching her fastestness. Stopped, both cling—staring at
            the corpse:
                plunge.

Cassy's eyes climb: gradually she upsurges; staring at Eliza,
    George does not move: gradually Eliza, straightening, raises
    her eyes—starts.
Cravingly erect, trembling; Cassy looks

simply Eliza holds out her doll
ghosteyes grope from the doll to Eliza and back again. George
does not move. Suddenly understanding—recognizing Eliza in
Eliza's child—Cassy opens starved arms
    trembling, Eliza rises: beside her rises George. Tenderly she
    dances, cradling her doll, toward Cassy: meanwhile he stands,
    erect; arms givingly outheld
daughter and mother cling. Kneeling before her daughter, Cassy
fondles the doll
    Eliza signs to George. Crossing his arms over his breast, he
    walks slowly to her and kneels; facing Cassy, who sees only
    the doll. Gently Eliza takes her mother's right hand in hers;
    Cassy looks up: Eliza places Cassy's hand on George's bowed
    head—timidly Cassy's mindeyes find the father of Eliza's
    child: alldrawing him wonderingly to herself, Cassy kisses
    George;
        Eliza kneels


Light


trumpets (forte)
    doll and man and woman fusingly become a silent golden
    pyramid
        —before the black curtains a black angel stands—


Trumpets (ff)
    deepening a silent keenness itself inclines:
        step by step, an inwardfacing stranger outmoves; at Tom's
        body the presence pauses: veiling a secret face, the darkness
        turns.
            Beckons

TRUMPETS (fff)
    and itself rhythmically collecting, Tom's body sprouts upward
    to face the angel: and its right arm drifts toward the angel's
        —two black hands touch—
            inward step by step moving, the anonymous darkness
            leads Tom's body toward black curtains, which part
            slightly; presence and shadow disappear: curtains close;
                silence
                  The earth's children bow to the earth


—SONG
    a vital immense triumphing sphere of sound, a luminously
    enormous world of alive voices, infinitely explodes; as
        blackness vanishes. Appear two mighty golden doors upon
        which blazes

LIGHT

outward goldenly slowly the huge doors open—revealing an
immeasurable radiance and which, prodigiously forthpouring
upon a stage drowned in glory, becomes angels in white robes
with harps of gold and crowns

· CURTAIN ·

# E. E. Cummings and the Theatre

NORMAN FRIEDMAN

Although chiefly known for his poetry, Cummings was quite prolific in a wide variety of genres—autobiographical narratives, critical essays, children's stories, surrealistic/comic prose, drawings, and paintings—and, of course, drama and dance. Among these last are four published works, the most significant of which is the first, a play entitled *Him,* published in November of 1927 and originally performed in April of 1928.

The action revolves around two principal characters, Him, a would-be playwright, and Me, his ladylove. As they are at an impasse in their relationship, so too is he at an impasse in his art; indeed, the two issues seem inextricably intertwined, because the difficulty with the play he is trying to write has much to do with the difficulty they have in getting past the roles they have been playing with each other—"lover" and "mistress"—and accepting their actual identities as complex human selves. For she is, as it seems, pregnant with his child but is reluctant to tell him for fear of seeming to entrap him—or even, perhaps, of spoiling an already fragile relationship.

As Cummings himself put it in a letter of 1961, "Him's deepest

wish is to compose a miraculously intense play-of-art—Me's underlying ambition is to be entirely loved by someone through whom
she may safely have a child. He loves,not herself,but the loveliness
of his mistress;she loves, not himself,but the possibility of making a husband out of a lover. For him,sexual ecstasy is a form of
selftranscendence:for her,it's a means to an end(motherhood)." Of
Me, he says, "She has 'no mind';but possesses something minutely
more powerful than either intellect or intelligence:the Intuition
whose triumph constitutes the play's final scene"—whose meanings
we shall come back to in due course.

The plot brings Him to realize the nature of his problem—that
he is unable to write his play because he is unable to love. And he is
unable to love because he doesn't know who he is and is therefore
unsure of himself. But coming to realize the nature of his problem
is not tantamount to being able to resolve it. And yet, realization is
resolution when formally considered, although it is a tentative and
ambiguous way to end a play. But faithful to an organicist aesthetic,
as will be shown below, Cummings is being natural and true to his
material in avoiding a pasted-on ending.

Delicate and complex as is the rendering of this plot, Cummings complicated it further by a number of unusual dramatic
and staging devices—unusual because, even in the avant-garde and
experimental twenties, it was so provocative that it aroused a storm
of controversy. Indeed, even in the post–World War Two period of
The Theatre of the Absurd, it was seen and appreciated as a precur-
sor and has been revived a number of times since then.

In a series of essays written about this same time, Cummings
explains his theory of art, and especially of drama. His basic principle is organicist: art is not *about* something, it rather *is* something,
"the cordial revelation of the fatal reflexive." This is in the tradition
of Coleridge's *natura naturans* as opposed to *natura naturata,* nature
in process rather than as product. A vision of this same principle

was adopted, in terms of their own program, by the New Critics in their notion of art as self-referring, and back to Oscar Wilde and the nineties, and even back to Kant and to Aristotle. So Cummings wrote in the original theatre program, "this PLAY isn't 'about', it simply is."

He means what Coleridge meant when he said that the content determines the form rather than being shaped by an arbitrarily predetermined form, and thus that form and content are not separable. Every successful work of art, therefore, is in certain ways unique: if form grows out of content, and if content is unique, then the form will vary as the content varies.

Cummings applied this principle to the theatre by requiring that audience and play be able to confront and interact with one another. The picture-frame stage is thus inorganic, mechanical, and sterile, for it persists in thrusting conventional illusion-making devices between performance and audience. The peep-show stage substitutes static surface for dynamic space, thus scene (surface) and actor (space) negate each other, and no organic cohesion is possible. In the "space-stage," on the other hand, the stage is empty, functioning as space; it has ceased to appeal as decoration. The play itself is required to give life to this space; everything now depends upon the play, which is no longer separated from the audience. Thus is created an organic relation between actors and stage, play and theatre, performance and audience.

The results are as follows. Cummings uses a room with a window and a mirror for the Him-Me scenes, but he rotates it four times during the course of the play, so that it ends where it began, with actors and audience confronting one another through the invisible mirror. Thus the audience sees the room as having four walls rather than three plus an illusory fourth. Additionally, Cummings makes symbolic play with window and mirror. But most of the other scenes—the surrealistic ones—are played in space rather than within any picture frame. In this way depth and movement are created.

Written into the action, however, are much more crucial devices, literary as much as theatrical. First, the central conflict between Me and Him is presented only by indirection, which is one of the reasons why the play is difficult to interpret. Cummings fashions the dialogue between these distraught lovers so that the audience only gradually discovers—organically—that the woman's pregnancy is threatening to cause their separation. Not simply dialogue but also recurring birth references serve to convey implicitly what is happening. Third, there is the framing device of the placard picturing a doctor anesthetizing a woman, and the climactic emergence of Me with a baby at the freak show near the end.

"This play of mine is all about mirrors," says Him toward the end of Act 1 (27). And speaking of framing devices, Cummings' play is also, in the fourth place, full of mirrorlike repetitions and symmetries. The Doctor, the one who is anesthetizing Me on the placard that serves as the backdrop for the choruslike Misses Weird scenes, keeps reappearing in different disguises throughout. He is called "a harmless magician," "a master of illusion," and "his name is Nascitur" (114). Fifth, the structure of Act 1 is balanced: two Him-Me scenes framed by three scenes involving the Misses Weird. And Act 3 is similarly, but more complexly, balanced. On the placard, furthermore, as the head of the woman is being anesthetized, her eyes close at the beginning of Act 1 and open again in the middle of the last act. And of course her baby is born at the end.

Doubling and balancing occur throughout. The second act consists of scenes from the play being written by the hero of Him's Play—the Man in the Mirror—who is writing a play about a man writing a play. The Gentleman (played by the Doctor) is just about to be reborn at the end of Act 2, thereby paralleling the birth of Me's baby at the end of Act 3. Both Him and Me are aware of other selves each has created in *place* of the other. All the characters of Act 2 reappear at the end of Act 3, thereby creating an intersection between the world of Him and Me and the Man in the Mirror's Play. And at the end, another such intersection occurs between actors and audience.

In Act 2, Scene 1, Him presents the Man in the Mirror's play to Me in the hope of improving her understanding of him. It consists of eight satirical scenes, the doctor playing a leading role in each. Scene 2: three drunken middle-aged men and a repressed old maid, 3: a snake oil vendor, 4: two business partners have turned into each other, 5: a Censor tries to halt a bawdy performance of "Frankie and Johnny," 6: an Englishman carrying his Unconscious in a steamer trunk is stopped by a suspicious detective, 7: two Babbitts aboard an ocean liner, 8: A burlesque "Roman" drama, and 9: a man is accosted by a hungry mob in the ruins of post–World War I Europe.

At the end of each of these displays, however, Me remains unimpressed. Him's attempts, therefore, to reunite his various selves and to explain himself to Me so far result in failure. Act III plays out this continuing impasse and concludes with a freak show (Scene 6) and a final Me-Him scene (Scene 7).

The freak show seems to represent a fantasy that Me is having as a result of the frustrating dialogue with Him which precedes it. The Barker, who is the Doctor in disguise, introduces each of nine freaks (one for each month of Me's pregnancy). The spectators are all characters from the Other Man's play in Act 2, plus the three Misses Weirds. The ninth and last freak is Princess Anankay (the Goddess of Necessity and the mother of the Three Fates), who turns out to be Me holding a newborn babe in her arms. The three Weirds cry, "It's all done with mirrors" and Him "utters a cry of terror" (125) at the sight. Blackout.

Three worlds are intersecting here: the sterile world of Him's play, the actual world of the lovers, and a third and new world—that of the freaks—each world complementing the other, thereby remedying the inner lack in each. The freaks represent life and vitality to Him (and to Cummings): as the ordinary world of most people looks grotesque to the artist, so too do real individuals look like freaks to the ordinary world. Thus the final freak of all, a woman and her baby, causes the crowd to recoil and the Misses Weird to turn up their noses in disgust.

Indeed, the "cry of terror" uttered by Him suggests that he is still caught in his *own* dilemma: the world of Me and the child has entered the world of his art and has transformed it—for this is what was missing—and yet he has been unable to effect this transformation within himself. This is borne out by the final scene. The room is now back where it started, with the invisible mirror between the play and the audience. But the mirror has become a window, as Me discovers, for she suddenly realizes that there are real people in the audience and that they are pretending this room and its occupants are real. Thus have art and life, play and audience, intersected. But Him can't believe it, and so remains to the very end frozen in the dilemma whose meaning he is just beginning to understand.


## II

Not published in separate book form until 1944, *Anthropos: or The Future of Art* first appeared in 1930 in an anthology, edited by Walter S. Hankel, entitled *Whither, Whither, or After Sex, What? A Symposium to End Symposiums.* Less a play than an exemplum or skit, *Anthropos* in some respects anticipates *Santa Claus.* The three politicians are Death, the artist is Santa, and the Mob is the mob. Although printed without formal divisions, the play falls naturally into three parts:

1. The scene, which remains the same throughout, is the inside of a cave. On the left are three infrahuman creatures dressed in filthy skins, on the right is a naked man drawing something on

the wall, and in the central background is a curtain of skins, outside of which can be heard the noise of a machine clanking. The action consists of two sets of events proceeding simultaneously: the three creatures are discussing something while the artist is constructing his design, neither side paying attention to the other. The three creatures, who are named "G," "O," and "D," respectively, are trying, in contemporary slang, to hit upon the proper slogan—for what purpose, we don't as yet know—and they are considering various alternatives. Meanwhile, the artist has made an elephantlike design that is not yet quite achieved.

2. The three creatures simultaneously hit upon "Ev. O. Lution" as their slogan, and they call in the mob to tell them. The mob is a crowd of infrahuman dwarfs, and they file down the center aisle of the audience and salute. The three creatures tell them that the war will soon be over, for evolution is their ally. The mob cheers and leaves.

3. The artist, who has been oblivious to all this, goes to the curtain of skins at the back of the stage. The three creatures, seeing him for the first time, are aghast. He says he's stuck and needs another look at the mammoth. They are incredulous, telling him that mammoths are extinct. He tears aside the curtain, revealing a steamshovel at work, and crawls out cautiously, as if he were stalking a dangerous animal. The three creatures shrink from the blinding sunlight and close the curtain.

A platonic parable with a difference, this play is Cummings' comment on the nature of reality. The point about the slogan-makers is that their "solution" is a complete non sequitur and yet that it works anyway, a perfect forecast of Madison Avenue's latest motivation research techniques, for the politician's problem is not so much to win the war as to make the mob *think* that the war is being won. There is nothing real here at all. On the other hand, the point of the artist's solution to his problem is simply that he has to go outside and take another look. The irony is that the object of his attention is itself a product of civilization, and yet to him it is a mammoth—something alive and kicking. And we may recall the Foreword to *is 5* (1926) where Cummings says, "It is with roses and locomotives . . . that my 'poems' are competing."

Although *Anthropos,* like Cummings' remaining plays, moves toward a more abstract form of presentation than *Him,* it is nevertheless experimental and once again engages the question of how to be an artist. But here Cummings has left behind the problem of marriage and children and is beginning to assume his characteristic stance of the Artist versus Society.

## III

*Tom* (1935) is a script for a ballet based on Harriet Beecher Stowe's *Uncle Tom's Cabin* (1852), and it is written as a combination of synoptic narrative and dance description. The ballet is divided into four episodes: *One.* George, a slave, is fleeing Haley, a slave trader who comes to the Shelbys' plantation. Haley is in possession of the Shelbys' mortgage and so forces them to sell Eliza, George's wife, and Tom. *Two.* While Eliza tries to escape with her baby over the ice floes, George is pursued by Haley's slave catchers, but they are both rescued by a group of Quakers. *Three.* Meanwhile, Haley is bringing Tom by StClare's New Orleans estate. Eva, StClare's ailing little daughter, is revived by the sight of Tom, and StClare buys him. Eva dies, however, as does her father; his slaves are then put up at auction, and Legree, the brutal master of Cassy, Eliza's mother, buys Tom. *Four.* Tom arouses Legree's wrath when they arrive at the latter's Red River plantation, and Legree beats him to death. Legree is then extinguished by the spirit of Creative Nature, who turns into Cassy. George, Eliza, and the child enter, are reunited with Cassy around Tom's body, and are surrounded by divine radiance in a final apotheosis, as Death disappears with Tom's body and the Heavenly Host appears.

All this is done in about thirty pages. A bird's-eye view of the action reveals an artfully balanced structure: One—George-Eliza, Tom. Two—George-Eliza. Three—Tom. Four—George-Eliza, Tom. This structure suits the stylized manner of its presentation, as well as the formal pattern of separation-reunion, escape-capture, death-redemption, which organizes the whole. The theme of the ballet is an allegorical demonstration of downtrodden Good triumphing over powerful Evil, and it turns on two redemptions. The first is of the deus ex machina sort, in Episode Two, in that the Quakers come from nowhere to rescue the helpless fugitives; while the second, in Episode Four, is more organic—indeed paradoxical where Good triumphs over Evil in being defeated by it. Regarding the manner of presentation, the narrative portions are written as pantomime,. while the dance portions are written as formal choreography. In both cases, however, gestures are assigned to symbolize character, and much use is made, as in *Him*, of light, darkness, and space. The language, finally, is equally stylized, making much use of verbal compounds in the effort to describe motion.

The chief difference between Cummings and Mrs. Stowe, apart from the fact that the novel is over five hundred pages, is that her purpose was more sociological-humanitarian, while his was primarily spiritual. In *Tom* it is not the institution of slavery that is under attack so much as Evil itself. And it is not so much being attacked as defeated: brute power must surrender at last to spiritual force.

## IV

There remains *Santa Claus*, subtitled *"A Morality,"* first published in the spring 1946 issue of *The Harvard Wake*, devoted to work by and about Cummings. The play came out in book form in December of that same year.

It is divided into five scenes. *Scene One*: The two actors playing the central roles are wearing costumes appropriate to each. Death "wears black tights on which the bones of his skeleton are vividly suggested by daubs of white paint; and his mask imitates crudely the face of a fleshless human skull." Santa Claus is "a prodigiously paunchy figure in faded red motheaten Santa Claus costume, with the familiar Santa Claus maskface of a bewhiskered jolly old man" (141). It is necessary to establish these details, for, as we shall see, they are involved in the turning points of the action.

Death is strolling, and Santa enters despondently. He is sick at heart, for he has "so much to give; and nobody will take" (141). It becomes apparent later that he has become separated from his wife and daughter. Death replies that *his* problem is just the reverse, for he has "so much to take; and nobody will give" (142). He explains to the incredulous Santa that people in this unworld simply can't take what is freely offered—in this case, understanding. On the other hand, knowledge, by contrast, can be easily sold, and he urges Santa to become a knowledge-salesman, a.k.a., a Scientist. When Santa protests that he *has* no knowledge, Death reassures him that "the less something exists, the more people want it" (144). He then exchanges his mask with Santa's: underneath his is a fleshless human skull, but underneath Santa's is the face of a young man. Santa can't think of anything to sell that doesn't exist, so Death suggests a wheelmine.

*Scene Two* shows Santa selling wheelmine stock to a crowd of people. Masked, we recall, as Death, he tells the Mob that Science will free them from their obscene humanity and make them all supermen, flattering them in order to sell more wheelmine stock, and he is quite successful. *Scene Three*: Something, however, has happened at the wheelmine in the interim, for some miners have been injured or killed in an accident there. Death, as in the first scene, is strolling, only this time he is masked as Santa. He hears angry voices, and he says in self-satisfaction, "I've got him now!" (148). Santa enters, masked as Death, running from the Mob, and again asks for help. Death assures him that wheelmines don't exist. Then how, asks Santa, can a wheelmine hurt people, turn them into monsters. Because, answers Death, *people* don't exist either. At this point, Santa suddenly realizes who Death really is, but he is desperate and still needs advice, so Death tells him that what he obviously must do is prove that he also (Santa) doesn't exist. Apparently, Death expects his advice to complete Santa's downfall, for the Mob fears Death and will never believe he (i.e., Santa masked as Death) doesn't exist.

Death exits, but as it turns out, he hasn't reckoned on the power of the little girl who follows the Mob, which has just reentered. Santa, who has now seen that he was tricked by Death, tries to explain to the Mob what's wrong:

> *Ladies and gentlemen: if you all have been*
> *deceived by some impostor—so have I. . . .*
> *—How should our sages miss the mark of life,*
> *and our most skillful players lose the game?*
> *your hearts will tell you, as my heart has told me:*
> *because all know, and no one understands.*
> *—O, we are all so very full of knowing*
> *that we are empty: empty of understanding.*

And in a last attempt to save his skin, he tells the Mob that he will "abide by the verdict of that little girl / over there, with the yellow hair and the blue eyes." Whoever she says he is, he will agree to be. The Mob consents, and the child says, "You are Santa Claus." The Mob laughs, "there ain't no Santa Claus!" So Santa is exonerated:

*Then, ladies and gentlemen, I don't exist.*
*And since I don't exist, I am not guilty.*
*And since I am not guilty, I am innocent.*
*—Goodbye! And, next time, look before you leap.* (150–151)

As it turns out, then, Death's advice inadvertently proved, as he says in the next scene, "efficacious" (151).

*Scene Four:* Santa, still masked as Death, is the one who is strolling this time, and he is wondering who that Child was. Death, still masked as Santa Claus, enters, and Santa thanks him for his good advice. Death now needs the rest of Santa's costume, as he has a date with a woman who prefers fat fellows, so they complete the exchange. At this point, the child enters and immediately recognizes Santa, in spite of his additional disguise. She explains that they are both looking for somebody very beautiful and very sad, somebody who is sad because she has lost them both.

*Scene Five:* The Woman enters, weeping, for "Knowledge has taken love out of the world / and all the world is empty empty empty" (154). She calls for death, for she has lost her joy and her love and herself. Santa, dressed as Death, enters and speaks; she becomes strangely happy, seeming to hear the voice of her love again. The Mob enters, reeling and capering, carrying on a pole the corpse of Death disguised as Santa Claus, exulting over having revenged themselves at last over Science, whom they identify with Santa Claus. Santa disguised as Death fooled them, but Death disguised as Santa didn't, and each time it was the Child who was instrumental in revealing the true identity of each. The play concludes with Santa unmasking and being reunited with the Woman and Child at last.

In sum, Death has taken over the world, and only three people remain free, but they have lost one another. Death tries to ensnare Santa but is foiled by the Child. He then heads for the Woman, for she is the one he has a date with, but is accidentally intercepted by the Mob, and the Child is thereupon ironically responsible for his death. The plot, then, of this play is that of the biter bit, or the tables turned, for Death is caught in his own trap. Until the last scene, however, Santa is alone and has lost his love. That is why he is so easily duped by Death and why his lament to the Mob is so ineffective. He cannot save himself, only the Child saves him; he cannot conquer Death, only the Child can do that. Understanding itself is powerless without love; Santa must become an entire and whole human being through love before his understanding can become effective.

Cummings has come a long way, via *Tom,* from *Him.* Although each work involves the problem of the human trinity—father, mother, child—*Santa Claus* is quite different from *Him,* with *Tom* coming somewhere in between. The unborn baby was the main precipitant of strife between lover and lady in *Him,* whereas here the child is the chief agent of salvation and reconciliation. There was a similar reconciliation scene at the end of *Tom,* but the child there was not the redeemer. Finally, the depiction of the Mob in *Santa Claus* resembles and carries further that in *Anthropos,* thus becoming a standard fixture in the drama of Cummings' psyche. It is possible that the limitation in his output for the theatre, despite his obvious talent and relish for the task, can be traced back to his reluctance in granting human credibility to those aspects of the human scene that he deplored—a restriction less disabling in lyric/satiric forms than in those of the theatre.

*—Flushing, NY*

[Portions of this essay were adapted, with permission, from my book, *E. E. Cummings: The Growth of a Writer,* chapters 4, 6, 9, and 11, copyright © 1964 by Southern Illinois University Press, Carbondale.]

# A Bibliography of Cummings
# and the Theatre

## PRIMARY WORKS

Cummings, E. E. *Him* (New York: Boni and Liveright, 1927. Reprinted. New York: Liveright, 1955, 1970).

————. *Anthropos: The Future of Art* (Mt. Vernon, NY: Golden Eagle Press, 1944).

————. *Anthropos: L'Avenir, de l'Art*. Trans. D. Jon Grossman (Paris: Le Temps qu'il fait, 1986).

————. *Tom* (New York: Arrow Editions, 1935).

————. Three Speeches from an Unfinished Play. *E. E. Cummings: A Miscellany Revised*. Ed. George J. Firmage (New York: October House, 1965). First pub. *The New American Caravan* (New York: W. W. Norton, 1936); *Partisan Review* (March 1938); *Furioso* (Summer 1921), and *This is My Best,* Whit Burnett, ed. (Garden City: Halcyon House, 1944, Dial Press, 1942), 812–17.

————. *Santa Claus: A Morality. Harvard Wake* 5 (Cummings Number, Spring 1946), 10–19. Rpt. New York: Holt, 1946.

————. *Le Père Noël (Une moralité)*. Trans. D. Jon Grossman (Paris: Privately Printed, 1982).

————. *Le Père Noël/Santa Claus*. Trans. D. Jon Grossman (Paris: L'Herne, 1998).

————. *i: six nonlectures* (Cambridge: Harvard University Press, 1953).

[Contains comments by Cummings himself on *Him, Tom,* and *Santa Claus* in nonlectures 4, 5, and 6.]

————. *Selected Letters of E. E. Cummings.* Ed. F. W. Dupee and George Stade (New York: Harcourt Brace Jovanovich, 1969) [Consult the index.]

————. *Three Plays and A Ballet.* Ed. George J. Firmage (New York: October House, 1967 and London: Peter Owen, 1968). [Contains the plays *Him, Anthropos, Santa Claus,* and the ballet *Tom.*]

## SECONDARY WORKS

Benedikt, Michael. "*Santa Claus* by E. E. Cummings." *Theatre Experiment* (Garden City: Doubleday, 1967), 73.

Dendinger, Lloyd. N., ed. *E. E. Cummings: The Critical Reception* (New York: Burt Franklin, 1981). [On *Him* 87–108, *Tom* 179–85]

Donaghue, Denis. "*Drame à Thèse: Auden* and Cummings [*Santa Claus*]." *The Third Voice* (Princeton: Princeton University Press, 1959), 70–75.

Dos Passos. John. "Mr Dos Passos on *Him.*" *New York Times,* 22 Apr. 1928, sec. 9, p. 2. Rpt. *The Major Nonfictional Prose.* Ed Donald Pizer (Detroit: Wayne State University Press, 1988). 110–111.

Dumas, Bethany K. *E. E. Cummings: A Remembrance of Miracles* (New York: Barnes & Noble, 1974). [Chapter 5 on all five works]

Esslin, Martin. *The Theatre of the Absurd* (Garden City: Anchor/Doubleday, 1961), xxii, 288–89; rev. ed. 1969, 8, 348–49.

Friedman, Norman. "HIM (1927)." *E. E. Cummings: The Growth of a Writer* (Carbondale: Southern Illinois University Press, 1964), 51–74

Grossman, Manuel L. "*Him* and the Modern Theatre." *Quarterly Journal of Speech* 54.3 (October 1968), 212–19.

Kaufman, Wolfe. "'Tom' as Ballet." *Variety* 120.11 (27 November 1936), 58.

Kennedy, Richard S. *Dreams in the Mirror: A Biography of E. E. Cummings* (New York: Liveright, 1980). [Chapters XVII (*Him*), XXV (*Tom*), XXVII (*Santa Claus*)]

Lozynsky, Artem. "An Annotated Bibliography of Works on Cummings."

*Journal of Modern Literature* 7.1 (1979), 350–93. [On *Him* 371–73, *Anthropos* 381, *Tom* 377, *Santa Claus* 380–81.

Maurer, Robert E. "E. E. Cummings' *Him.*" *Bucknell Review* 6 (May 1956), 1–27. Rpt. *E. E. Cummings: A Collection of Critical Essays.* Ed. Norman Friedman (Englewood Cliffs: Prentice-Hall, 1972), 133–55.

Norman, Charles. "The Poet as Playwright." *E. E. Cummings, The Magic Maker.* Rpt. (Boston: Little, Brown, 1972), 202–35.

North, Michael. *The Dialect of Modernism: Race, Language, and Twentieth Century Literature* (Oxford: Oxford University Press, 1994).

Rotella, Guy, ed. *Critical Essays on E. E. Cummings* (Boston: G. K. Hall, 1984). [Consult Index]

Seldes, Gilbert, et al. *"him" and the Critics: A Collection of Opinions on E. E. Cummings' Play at The Provincetown Playhouse* (New York: Province-town Playhouse, 1928).

Smeltsor, Marjorie. "'Damn Everything but the Circus': Popular Art in the Twenties and *Him.*" *Modern Drama* 17 (1974), 43–55.

Strickland, William Franklin "E. E. Cummings' Dramatic Imagination: A Study of *Three Plays and a Ballet,*" Ph.D. diss., University of Florida, 1973.

Wagner-Martin, Linda. "Cummings' *HIM*—and Me." *Spring* New Series 1 (1992), 28–36.

Wegner, Robert E. *The Poetry and Prose of E. E. Cummings* (New York: Harcourt, Brace & World, 1965). [On *Him* 26–36; on *Anthropos* 134–41]

Wilson, Edmund. "E. E. Cummings' *Him,*" *The Shores of Light* (New York: Farrar, Straus and Young, 1952. 282–85. [This is a review of the play as published.]

Worth, Katherine J. "Poets in the American Theatre," *American Theatre.* Stratford-upon-Avon Studies. No. 10. Ed. John Russell Brown and Bernard Harris (London: Edward Arnold, 1967). 102–7.

Young, Stark. *"Him" New Republic,* LIV (May, 2, 1928), 325–26. Rpt in S. V. Baum, ed. *EΣTI:eec: E. E. Cummings and the Critics.* East Lansing: Michigan State University Press, 1962, 47–49. [This is a review of the play as performed.]

## PERFORMANCES OF CUMMINGS' WORKS

### HIM

Provincetown Playhouse, Macdougal Street, NYC, April–May, 1928, James Light, director, with Erin O'Brien-Moore, William S. Johnstone, and Lawrence Bolton in the leads.

Provincetown Playhouse, Summer 1948, The Interplayers, Irving Stiber, director, with Janet Shannon, John Denny, and Gene Saks.

Eric Bentley, Salzburg, 1950: see *"Him* (1929)," *From the Modern Repertoire: Series Two.* Ed. Eric Bentley (Denver: Denver University Press, 1952), 485–94.

The Rectangle Theatre, NYC, 1956.

Circle Repertory Theatre, 2307 Broadway, NYC, April 1974, Marshall Oglesby, director, with Trish Hawkins, Lanford Wilson, and Neil Flanagan.

University of California at Berkeley: see William I. Oliver, *"Him*—A Director's Note," *Educational Theatre Journal* 26.3 (October, 1974), 327–41.

Hyperion Theatre Group, The Vineyard Theatre, E. 26th Street, NYC, July–August, 1983, Gregg Goldstone, director, with Catherine Baier, Richard Mover, and Kevin O'Leary.

Medicine Show, E. 2nd Street, NYC, April–May 1991, Barbara Vann, director, with John McIlveen, Cori Thomas, and Norton Banks.

Viaduct Theater, Chicago, IL, May–June 2005, Whitney Blakemore, director.

### SANTA CLAUS

No direct evidence of performances of this play has come my way, but there are reports that it was performed in Iowa City sometime between 1954 and 1959, in NYC at the Gate Theatre during spring–summer 1960, and at the Theatre de Lys in NYC during the early 1960s.

## TOM

David Diamond, Suite No. 1, from the Ballet *Tom,* The Waterloo Festival Orchestra, Gerard Schwarz, conductor, Carnegie Hall, NYC, May 11, 1985. First performed at a Waterloo Festival Concert, July 4, 1981.

*The Enormous Room,* adapted for the stage by The Next Theatre Company of Evanston, IL, Noyes Cultural Arts Center, February–March, 1989, John Carlisle, director.

## THE AUTHOR AND HIS WORK

"E. E. Cummings: The Making of a Poet," a self-portrait, told by the poet in his own voice, with his poetry, paintings, and notebooks; filmstrip; Films for the Humanities, Harold Mantell, Princeton, NJ; introduced at The Museum of Modern Art, NYC, by Stanley Kunitz, November 9, 1971.

## PERFORMANCE THEATRE BASED ON POEMS

"Americans: A Portrait in Verses," CBS News Television, August, 16, 1962, four poems by Cummings performed-recited, among others by Sandburg, Fearing, Dickinson, Whitman, etc.

Cummings and Bowings, The U.R.G.E.N.T. Group, Quintana Roo Productions, West 46th Street, NYC, Nathan George, director, with music by Ravel, Hindemith, Honegger, Kodaly, and Ives, August 1973.

"Damn Everything But the Circus!", one-man show by William Mooney, Henry Kaplan, director; Washington DC, spring 1975; Central Michigan University, winter 1983; Gainesville, FL, spring 1984.

"Damn Everything but the Circus!", Masque Ensemble, Poetry Festival at St. Clements, West 46th Street, NYC, Loyd Williamson, director, fall 1979.

"Let's Start a Magazine," performed and produced by Hard Werken of Rotterdam, Ton Lutgerink, director, La Mama ETC, East 4th Street, NYC, spring 1983.

"Cummings and Goings," music by Ada Janik, Cooper-Hewitt Museum, East 91st Street, NYC, August 1983; Top of the Gate, Bleecker Street, NYC, February–March 1984.

"Damn Everything but the Circus!", Your Theatre, Inc., staged by Robert Saures, New Bedford, MA, October 1983.

"Viva. Cummings!", conceived and composed by Stephen F. Scotti, directed and choreographed by William A. Finlay, Boston University Playwrights Theatre and The New Stillington Players, Gloucester, MA, October 1984; Provincetown Inn, May 1990; presented by the Blue Heron Theatre, Inc., at the Mazur Theatre, East 90th Street, NYC, October 1990; Bogotá, Colombian, and Caracas, Venezuela, April 1992.

"e.e.," The California Stage Company, produced by Denis Wilkerson, directed by Edward Trafton, California State University, Sacramento, 1987; and at the S. Street Theatre, October 1991.

"UNREALITIES," Real Productions, Jose Fernandez-Chinea, director, Eric Gustaf Nord, composer, David Maurice Sharp, choreographer, November 1989 and March 1992, NYC.